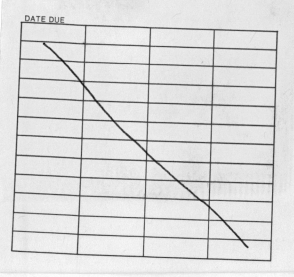

The Art of Paul Verlaine

THE ART OF

Paul Verlaine

By *ANTOINE ADAM*

Translated by Carl Morse

NEW YORK UNIVERSITY PRESS 1963

The original French edition of this book appeared under the title Verlaine *and was published by Hatier, Paris.*

CONTENTS

Part One · *LIFE*

Part Two · *WORKS*

The Art of Paul Verlaine

Part One · Life

1 · *Before Rimbaud*

Verlaine was born in Metz on March 30, 1844. His father's name was Nicolas-Auguste Verlaine. Adjutant battalion captain of the 2nd Regiment of the Engineering Corps, he was forty-six years old when his son was born. His mother's name was Elisa Dehée. She was not thirty-two but thirty-five years old in 1844, having been born on March 23, 1809. His parents were married in Arras on December 15, 1831.

At birth the child was given the first names Paul and Marie. He was the first born and remained an only child. Before his birth Madame Verlaine had hoped on three other occasions to become a mother and had been disappointed each time. If the poet's account is accurate, she had preserved the memory of her triple disappointment in three jars.

The Verlaines were an old family from the Ardennes region of Belgium, and notary records enable us to trace its history from the sixteenth century. The poet's grandfather was a notary in Bertrix. His wife, a Grandjean, on becoming a widow retired nearby in Jehonville. One of her sisters lived in Paliseul. Le Fefve de Vivy's useful researches have revealed that Verlaine the notary had by his extreme views, the violence of his speech, and his insobriety, acquired a deplorable reputation. But it is no less important to note how strongly traditionalist and Christian in conviction and custom his and his wife's family were. Clerical families, one is almost tempted to say. The Grandjean family included nine priests, all close relatives of the

3

captain. And one notes among Verlaine's friends a professor at
the University of Louvain, a vicar-general of Namur, and a
director of the Grand Séminaire of the same town. It was for a
long time not known that these priests played a decisive role in
the poet's life, especially in times of crisis.

The Dehée family was originally from the Artois district.
Recent investigations, the results of which were printed in the
Revue des sciences humaines, have finally enabled us to know
the Dehées better. They were, in the eighteenth century,
olieurs, or oil-makers, established in Arras. Around 1742 they
moved to the village of Fampoux, a few miles away. There they
owned land and a mill "for the purpose of pressing oil." At the
time of the Revolution, Verlaine's great-grandfather, Pierre-
Joseph Dehée, was listed on the roster of large farm owners in
the district. Whereas the eldest of his children carried on the
trade of oil-maker in Arras, another son, Julien-Joseph, became a
farmer in Fampoux. Elected public magistrate in the Year IV
[1795], he remained mayor of the commune until 1803. Elisa,
the poet's mother, was Julien-Joseph Dehée's daughter. The
family was unquestionably respectable. It is curious to note,
however, that one of Elisa's cousins, Pierre-François Dehée, is
described in a police record of 1867 as "one of those idle persons,
of little learning and less knowledge, who thinks he can do anything he likes in the commune of Fampoux: a man as dangerous
in attitude as in conduct." When he spent his vacations in
Fampoux, Verlaine undoubtedly saw a good deal of this alarming cousin.

Both the Verlaines and the Dehées were financially comfortable. Captain Nicolas Verlaine possessed a capital of 400,-
000 francs. Bad investments caused him to lose a part of his
fortune, but his sister-in-law claims that in 1870 Elisa Verlaine still had 200,000 francs. A female cousin of the future
poet had married the owner of an important sugar factory in
Lécluse, who, according to Verlaine, earned 80,000 francs a
year from making cane sugar out of his beets.

The captain was tall, lean, and erect, with a military air and
an habitually stern look. He gave the impression of being very
stubborn, a little severe and grumpy. Was he, as certain ob-
servers have thought, so strict as to inspire awe in his son? Or

was he, on the contrary, as his family claimed, indulgent to the point of weakness with this difficult child? One thing is certain—that he made himself deeply loved by that child.

Elisa Dehée was physically a rather tall woman with a pleasant, delicately-featured face. Officer's wife and landowner's daughter, she deliberately affected a cold dignity. But Germain Nouveau, who saw her over a long period of time in Arras, said she was gay as a finch and lively as gunpowder. Ernest Delahaye, too, spoke of her in discerning and judicious terms. She was, he said, affectionate, childish, and rash. The Belgian Verlaines did not like her. They said she was not very bright, and that she was flighty and superstitious. She was perhaps somewhat more than thrifty, and her daughter-in-law maintained that under the surface of a proper middle-class lady she concealed the basic nature of a greedy and rancorous old peasant woman. But history will retain the memory of her infinite patience and long martyrdom that was to end in her wretched death in the slum of the Cour Saint-François.

CHILDHOOD AND YOUTH

Up until 1851, Captain Nicolas Verlaine changed his residence several times. He was stationed in Montpellier. He was in Nîmes when the riots of 1848 broke out. Little Paul followed him in these changes of abode. The captain came back to Metz and was there when he resigned from the army. We do not know the motive behind this decision: it seems he wanted very much to live in Paris and that he threw over his career as an officer when it became clear that he could expect to end his days in a provincial garrison. After turning in his resignation, he went to live in the Batignolles section of Paris.

In 1853, young Paul was entrusted to the care of the Institution Landry at 32 Rue Chaptal. He stayed there nine years (1853–1862). Entering when he was nine, he first took his elementary classes there; then, beginning in 1855, like the other pupils of the institution, he attended classes at the Lycée Bonaparte, now the Lycée Condorcet.

If we wish to picture him at this period of his life, we should begin by dismissing the account in his *Confessions*. In it Verlaine relates only insignificant anecdotes. He also makes allegations in which it is difficult to distinguish between the part played by humility and that by boastfulness, and in which one unquestionably detects a good deal of posing. He had been a delightful and willful child. Up to the age of ten he refused to sleep if his mother was not nearby. He loved to play close by his parents and spent hours drawing. He delighted the entire family, we are told, because he was so affectionate and loving. One forgot he wasn't good-looking. One forgave his whims. He grew up surrounded by the adoration of his mother and of a cousin, Elisa Moncomble, whom Madame Verlaine was raising in her home, an orphan eight years older than Paul who spoiled the little boy. The authority of his father was thereby somewhat weakened. It is probable—and it was said at Paliseul and Jehonville—that the captain sent Paul to boarding school at the age of nine because he had become "impossible."

Later Verlaine boasted of having been a very poor student at the lycée. A look at his position in his class during these seven years makes the truth clear. Up to the ninth grade he worked with application and success. But from then on one observes a falling-off that becomes even more marked in the course of the next two years. In his sophomore year he stops working even in his favorite subjects, Latin and French. In his junior year he fluctuates between twentieth and fiftieth place in a class of fifty-nine pupils—he who at the end of the eighth grade had been sixth in a class of seventy-one. It took the prospect of his *baccalauréat* exams to settle him down to more earnest effort in his final year, his "rhetoric year." He received his *baccalauréat* diploma on August 16, 1862. He wrote to a friend at the time that in order to pass he had "worked like a black." But a failing mark in physics just missed jeopardizing this last-minute recovery.

If we consult other factual records, pictures of Verlaine dating from this period, they confirm the conclusions that emerge from the child's school record. A photograph taken in 1857 shows a little boy much less ugly than he is said to have been, a boy who looks well-behaved and thoughtful. Another photograph shows him as a lycée student. The forehead is high, the face—which is elongated—is not without distinction. The eyes, especially, are

interesting: pensive, and one could easily say, ardently solemn.
But then, around the age of fifteen, his physical appearance
changes—just as his marks in school changed. A drawing by
Cazals, made at a later date from a photograph taken in 1859,
shows a cynical-looking and unpleasantly ugly schoolboy. The
same impression is given by another drawing made from a
photograph taken in 1860. One can see what was meant by the
description of his junior-year teacher (the historian Perrens):
"a hideous mug that reminded one of a hardened criminal . . .
the most slovenly pupil in person and dress at the Lycée Bonaparte."

Verlaine has told us that he lost his faith in the years following his First Communion. Let us accept this as true. But what he
does not report is that he continued to go to confession and,
whenever he was with his family, to fulfill his religious duties.
Edmond Lepelletier, one of his schoolmates at the lycée, maintains that he no longer believed in God. But he has to admit
that his friend attended the sermons of Father Monsabré and
Father Minjard. One bit of verse, "Aspiration," written by the
young lycée student in 1861, expresses his preoccupation with
religion. A letter of the following year gives evidence of a freshness of soul, of a rather naïve idealism, and of a still keen moral
sense.

From all of this evidence one discerns the direction in which
the young man developed. It was not right after his First Communion, it was when he was already a ninth-grade student and
fourteen years old that he so radically changed, that he became
the skeptical and derisive schoolboy he spoke of later. He spent
his time reading obscene books and perhaps writing filthy verses.
But, at bottom, he kept intact his dream of childish innocence,
a nostalgia for lost purity which was linked with his home life—
to the love in which an admired and cherished father and
mother enveloped him, and to the traditions of dignity and
morality he had observed in both his Ardennes and his Artois
relations. Curiously enough, one of his lycée schoolmates had
detected this dual personality in the young man, these opposing
forces drawing him toward the ideal and toward filth. A drawing he did at the time shows Paul Verlaine as an "astronomer

(*sic*) falling into a sewer." The future poet of *Parallèlement*
(*Parallelly*) is already characterized in this caricature and its
caption.

BEFORE MARRIAGE

Having finished his *baccalauréat*, Verlaine began to study
law with a view to taking the entrance examination for the
ministry of finance. He enrolled in the law school and took
several courses in French and Roman law. But he found the
hours spent in the "dives" of Rue Soufflot more enjoyable. His
lack of interest in his courses disturbed his father. He let it be
known everywhere that it was necessary to "find Paul a job."
He kept him at home for six months. A retired officer friend
found the young man a temporary job with the Amalgamated
Aigle and Soleil Insurance Company on Rue du Helder. He
stayed there just so long as it took him to get a job in the offices
of the Seine District Prefecture. First employed in the mayoralty
of the Ninth Arrondissement, Rue Drouot, he then went on to
the Hôtel de Ville. His work consisted of sending out the sal-
aries of the Paris clergy. A joyless but undemanding labor. His
workday, which started late, was broken by a two-hour lunch
period and ended at four o'clock. He was an indifferent forward-
ing agent and did not even bother to take the very easy tests
that would have permitted him to fill a less subordinate position.
He ended up as a draft clerk. On these first jobs he had earned
1,800 francs a year.

His father's health had become poor. The captain had long
suffered from rheumatism of the joints. In June and July of 1862
he was gravely ill. In March 1863, he contracted a cataract of
the left eye; the other eye was threatened. One day he had an
unfortunate fall. Several attacks of apoplexy followed which, in
less than two years, brought him to the grave. On December 30,
1865, a stroke carried him off. Paul and his mother went to live
in a much more modest apartment at 26 Rue Lécluse.

This period, which begins in 1863 and runs to 1869, is a critical one. Invaluable information comes to us from Belgium.
Verlaine had often spent his lycée vacations there and continued to make short stays in Paliseul and Jehonville. He had good
friends there—J.-B. Dewez, who later became a priest, and

Hector Perrot, whose family was very close to his own. He saw his elderly aunts there, Aunt Grandjean and Aunt Evrard. These good people worried about him. In September 1863, Father Delogne, formerly curate at Paliseul and recently appointed dean at Bouillon, wrote about him: "My little friend came to see me. I talked with him for a long time. His basic nature, I believe, has remained good. I have all the more basis for forming an opinion on the subject since he admitted several weaknesses to me and disclosed his fear of Paris. The big city is little suited to his feeble will!" But at that time the captain persisted in wanting a brilliant career for his son and could conceive of such a one only in Paris. After his death no decision was made.

Above all, let us not picture a young independent who has calculatingly decided to live life intensely and who has thrown over moral standards believing them all a swindle. Verlaine at this period is the very model of a good young man turning bad, one who lacks willpower and is unable to resist certain temptations. The oversolicitous upbringing he has had is bearing its fruit. His wife will speak of it later in terms that are not ungraphic. Paul's mother, she said, had got her son into the habit of sleeping in a flannel nightcap, like an old man or an invalid. She bundled him up in unsightly mufflers. When he went out, she smothered him with instructions: watch out for traffic, unfrequented streets, buildings under construction. She treated him like a six-year-old and, said the disillusioned wife, had made her son a cowardly, egotistical, and ridiculous creature. Verlaine at the time wrote to a friend: "You know me, replete with flannel, mufflers, cotton in my ears." Without knowing it, he was in this sentence corroborating Mathilde's grievances.

His comrades did not perhaps suspect just how far these spoiled-child oddities went. They considered him, according to Lepelletier's report, the most pleasant and likeable of chums. There is little if any reason to doubt his testimony. When Sivry spoke to his sister Mathilde of his friend Verlaine, he described him in these terms: "He is a very gentle and very kind fellow who adores his mother, with whom he lives." Delahaye, too, who knew the poet in 1871, spoke of his gentleness and of the ease with which he yielded to the will of others.

But two traits intrude to modify this picture of a mild and kind young man. First of all, he is subject to sudden and morbidly violent fits of anger. It is Delahaye again who reports these unpredictable rages in his friend. Verlaine, he said, yielded often and for long periods of time. Then suddenly, weary of submitting to the will of others, he became irritated and lashed out with the force of an overwound spring. At such times, especially, Verlaine took to drink.

He had begun drinking, according to Lepelletier, in 1863. Between the Hôtel de Ville and the distant Batignolles district, there were a great number of cafés in which to stop and refresh oneself. The young clerk never lacked for pocket money since his father gave him half of his pension for entertainment. In point of fact, however, it is probable that bad habits did not become ingrained and acquire their terrible aspect until some time later. Verlaine has said that two events had deeply upset him: the death of his father in 1865, and in February 1867 that of his cousin Elisa, which was wholly unexpected. He had doubtless very much loved this young woman who had been an older sister or a kind of very young mother to him. He recalled her later as

> *Blonde et rose, au profil pourtant grave et rêvant*
> *Avec de beaux yeux bleus . . .*
>
> Pink and blond, yet, in profile, dreaming, solemn
> With beautiful blue eyes . . .

He never forgot her "voice of living gold," her "fresh, angelic timbre," and according to J. H. Bornecque, a kind of romance sprang up between the young man and his married cousin: a great ill-fated love of which the *Poèmes saturniens (Saturnine Poems)* were to be the echo. She had married a man named Dujardin, the owner of a sugar mill in Lécluse. She died a few days after a lying-in. Verlaine, notified too late, arrived in Lécluse just as the funeral procession was starting for the cemetery. It was right after this calamity, he said, that he began drinking absinthe to excess and no longer drank the beer with which he had contented himself up to that point.

But one should bear in mind that aside from these crises Verlaine is a young man of sensitive feeling and lofty interests.

He assiduously follows the Pasdeloup concerts and goes to
museums and art exhibitions. He associates with colleagues at
the Hôtel de Ville—Mérat, Valade, Armand Renaud—who are
passionately fond, as is he, of poetry. His correspondence with
Lepelletier shows him hungry for culture and gives evidence
that he continues to bring moral concern to his readings. He
is not much given to diversion. One never sees him walking
with a lady on his arm. Is it true, as Delahaye claims, that he
suffered an unhappy passion for a young redhead? Is it true that
he was loved by a pretty Hungarian lady who left him indifferent? It is certain that women occupied little place in his life.
When by chance he let himself be taken to a party where vulgar
pleasures were in order, he grew bored and could not help looking glum. He had warm friendships with the young men of his
acquaintance. A cousin in Lécluse has been mentioned; people
have spoken of a Lucien Viotti. It should be clearly understood
that no one knows anything about the nature of these friendships, that no one has the right to imply they were impure, and
that the opposite is much more likely. When his senses called
too strongly, Verlaine allayed them in undistinguished adventures. One cannot positively state, although it is possible to
suspect, that these were not necessarily with women.

Seeing him with his friends one would undoubtedly find him
a very steady fellow, a little reticent perhaps, but gay enough.
And one would perhaps be right. It is more likely, however,
that this steadiness and gaiety conceal real anguish. The illness
and death of his father, and the death of Elisa, have deeply
affected the young man. He suffers from his ugliness and feels
himself a solitary. How, other than by this hidden sadness, can
one explain his taste for macabre humor, the lugubrious turn
his banter so readily takes, and especially the homicidal rages
that overcome him when drunk?

Verlaine, in 1869, was completely demoralized. In a letter in
July he says he is suffering terribly, that he is in the depths of a
horrible depression, and that he is incapable of writing verse.
He openly acknowledges the lamentable state of his nerves.
Moreover, he spoke later in a letter to Victor Hugo of the happy
and tranquil course his life took after marriage—"after excruci-
ating agonies." An affecting choice of words, one that leads one

to suspect an extremely painful crisis during the period preceding his engagement.

The most definite evidence we have for this period comes
again from the Ardennes country. At the beginning of June
Verlaine's *Correspondance* informs us that he left Paris suddenly because he was ill; he went to Fampoux to take a rest.
But a letter written by a woman from the Ardennes area on
July 18 reveals that actually the young man must have gone
away following an altercation in a café, and that having left on
sudden impulse, he returned four days later on another impulse.
Some weeks later, a new crisis. One time he came home at five
in the morning, drunk. He attacked his mother, screaming that
he was going to kill her and then kill himself. Madame Verlaine
dispatched a wire to her sister Marie-Rose Dehée. She was a
forceful woman whom her nephew held in awe. He remained
calm during the two days she spent in Paris. But two days later,
he was off again. He came home at one o'clock in the morning
with a friend. He again threatened his mother; he brandished
a sword over her head. The woman from Ardennes, Victoire
Bertrand, who was present, wrenched the sword away from
him, aided by his unknown companion. It was only after eight
hours of raging madness that calm was restored. Again Madame
Verlaine took her son to Fampoux; an illness was invented to
serve as an excuse for this new departure. "I believe," wrote
Victoire Bertrand, "that if he goes on this way, he will commit
a crime one of these days."

The family began to take heed. On March 22 Aunt Grandjean in Paliseul had died. Paul had arrived the following day.
His behavior on this occasion was so outrageous that they had
decided to take action. At the beginning of April they had
called him back on the pretext of settling details of the estate.
His relatives, friends, the parish priest, the notary had all agreed
to give him a good dressing-down. They urged him to get married to someone in the locality and to settle down there. He
seemed to agree. He made confession. A young cousin whose
"strength of character" was known had been proposed. The very
thought of facing this cousin made him decide to ask for the
hand of a young girl he had hardly seen, the half-sister of his
good friend Charles de Sivry.

THE ENGAGEMENT

These facts, which have been known only for the last thirty years, shed light on the account Verlaine left of his engagement. They enable one to judge the degree to which he simplified and consequently distorted his disclosure of the facts. The gesture that he described as completely spontaneous meant to him, at least to begin with, a way of escaping a scheme he wanted no part of.

The Mautés were natives of Nogent-le-Rotrou. Verlaine claimed that his father-in-law was a former provincial notary. But the daughter dismisses this honorable title as if it were an insult. The family had pretensions and had taken to calling themselves Mauté de Fleurville. They lived in a two-story house at 14 Rue Nicolet. An iron fence and a little garden separated it from the street. A door at the side for visitors, a large door for carriages, and two detached buildings serving as stable and coach house lent to the whole the look of a private mansion.

We know nothing of Théodore Mauté except through his daughter's and his son-in-law's descriptions. According to the former he was worldly, fond of hunting, dancing, and often away from home—and Mathilde does not hesitate to speak of his "habitual selfishness." Verlaine, who detested him, saw his father-in-law as "a pretentious and narrow-minded bourgeois, as besmattered with arty and literary notions as a crouton in a salad is with garlic." On the other hand, he was all his life to retain a very tender memory of the lady who was for a few years his mother-in-law, "the best and most intelligently broad-minded of women," he wrote. What he does not say but what one may easily guess is that the father was a puppet of a man whose formal bearing ill disguised his weakness, and that the decisions in the Mauté family were made by the mother and daughter.

The latter's name was Mathilde. She was born in Nogent-le-Rotrou on April 17, 1853. When Verlaine met her in 1869, she was sixteen years old. She was probably pretty and gave the impression of being intelligent because she played the piano, scrawled notebooks full of drawings, and composed doggerel-type verses. For a year now her half-brother, Charles de Sivry, had been taking her to Nina de Callias', and she often visited

a family of sculptors, the Bertaux. In the course of a visit to Rue
Nicolet, where he had gone to see Charles de Sivry, Verlaine
noticed the young girl for the first time. Some weeks later he
wrote to Sivry from Fampoux (where he had returned after the
dreadful scene reported by Victoire Bertrand) to inform him
of his desire to marry his half-sister. Sivry replied that he might
hope and came himself to spend several days in Fampoux. After
vacation, in October 1869, Verlaine called formally at Rue
Nicolet. His proposal was accepted.

One wonders what was behind this astonishing decision.
Some have explained the Mautés' attitude by considerations of
financial advantage. Unmoneyed middle-class people, they may
have been glad to marry off their daughter to a young man who
was an only son and who had "handsome prospects." That,
however, is doubtless unjust. Rather than selfish motivations,
one may discern an act of thoughtlessness. Mathilde is a spoiled
child whose head is turned by the glory of poets. She doesn't
even see her fiancé's ugliness, but only the fine, lithe, unassuming, distinguished figure he cuts, even as Delahaye will see it
two years later. She has heard it said that the young man will
one day be famous. She enlists her mother's aid, and the combined forces of these two irrational and charming women over-
ride the father's objections. The latter had declared that he
would not consent before his daughter was nineteen or twenty
years old. This resolve was not kept. It was agreed that the marriage would take place in June of 1870.

Whatever the young man's feelings may have been at the
outset, he showed himself to be very smitten, and his resolve to
behave properly again was sincere. Even according to Mathilde's
testimony he was "sweet, tender, affectionate, and gay" throughout the whole engagement period. He made an effort to stop
swearing. For all practical purposes, he had ceased to frequent
cafés. On one occasion at least he got drunk: but he managed,
at any rate, to conceal this lapse. Every Tuesday he entertained
his best friends at home. Victoire Bertrand saw Coppée, Valade,
L.-X. de Ricard, the Cros brothers, and Lepelletier there. Toward the end of 1869 Mathilde began to attend these gatherings.
Chabrier and Sivry played the piano. At some point during her

engagement to the poet, if one may believe her *Mémoires*, Villiers read *Elën* and *Morgane* in her presence: a rather astonishing assertion since *Elën* had been published in January 1865 and *Morgane* in March 1866. Verlaine recorded his love, his resolves, his dream of a return to happy and peaceful life in *La Bonne Chanson (Song of the Good)*.

At first the marriage was set for June 29, 1870. But the ceremony was postponed because Mathilde was ill. Then Madame Mauté fell sick in turn. The prenuptial contract was made on the twenty-third and twenty-fourth of June in the office of Taupin, who was notary in Clichy. It is important to take note of the principal clauses of this contract. It was based on the system of joint estate restricted to property acquired in common. Verlaine brought 20,000 francs worth of assets, 6,960 francs from the inheritance of his Aunt Grandjean, and a dowry of 20,000 francs settled on him by his mother as an advance on his inheritance. Mathilde's contribution was paltry: 4,200 francs in capital, furniture and linen valued at 5,794 francs, jewels and gifts valued at 1,200 francs, and 50 francs worth of 3 percent bonds. It is true, however, that the Mautés promised, unofficially, to give the young couple a sum annually, equal to that earned by Verlaine at the Hôtel de Ville. According to Mathilde, her husband's salary amounted at the time to 3,000 francs a year. Doubled by the amount to be contributed by the bride's parents and augmented by the earnings of Paul's capital, this income assured the young household a very comfortable living. And future prospects were excellent. Verlaine might later expect, upon the death of his mother, to come into an income of 10,000 francs a year.

MARRIAGE   THE WAR   THE COMMUNE

The marriage almost did not take place. War had broken out. News of the first calamities had just come. Paris had begun to stir. On August 10, a draft was called of all unmarried men in the class of 1864, which was Verlaine's class. But the fact that the banns had already been posted and the marriage date already set was allowed for. On the following day, August 11, Verlaine and Mathilde were married. The poet Valade was

witness for the groom. Paul Foucher was witness for Mathilde.
The young couple settled at 2 Rue du Cardinal-Lemoine in a
very nice apartment overlooking Quai de la Tournelle.

The Siege of Paris began. Those who insist on seeing Verlaine's life as no more than a long succession of immoralities
are loath to acknowledge that he was at one point responsive
to the call of patriotism. Although he could have avoided any
kind of active participation in the defense, he enlisted in the
160th Batallion and stood guard on the battlements between
Montrouge and Vanves. He had a streak of naïveté, of heed-
lessness, or as Stendhal would have said, *espagnolisme*. He knew
it, and in his letters he had already spoken of his craziness and
"harum-scarum ways." And again of himself as "never weary
of being heedless and simple-minded." But these bursts of
heroism didn't last. The long hours spent in the damp and cold
very quickly became unbearable to him. He tried to back out.
Then he actually became ill. This has been denied, but without
foundation, and a letter from Verlaine to Victor Hugo in December 1870 speaks of his throat as being "literally in flames."

Unfortunately his bad habits returned. Verlaine began to
drink again. There were a few scenes—rare, however, and not
violent. Opportunities were frequent and excuses offered themselves freely: idleness, boredom, the interminable stints in the
mud and snow of the battlements. Once during the winter
Mathilde went home to her mother. Then she forgave and came
back. Moreover, the household did not lack for pursuits that
contributed to good feeling. They entertained a great deal; they
received the Cros brothers, Régamey, Pelletan, Villiers, Valade,
Cabaner. And they went out—to the Burtys who lived behind
the Gobelins, and Mathilde was proud to find herself in the
company of Edmond de Goncourt, Ernest d'Hervilly, and
Bracquemond.

The group made up of Verlaine and his friends was one of
patriots. They hated not only the Empire but the conservative
forces, those self-styled elites who had just plunged the country
into the most desperate kind of peril. Bazaine and the partisans
of capitulation, the vainglorious and ineffectual officer's corps,
were loathsome to these good men—and the spectacle of the
ineffectuality and cowardliness of the civil powers had given

them a revolutionary turn of mind. Even before the war Verlaine was an Hébertist and found the Jacobins lukewarm. Thus, when the events of the Commune erupted, his heart was with the aroused populace. Just as were Mérat, Lepelletier, Blémont, and Louis-Xavier de Ricard. Emile Bergerat has reported that at Lemerre's he saw Verlaine advocate the Commune and laud the men of the Hôtel de Ville. He also saw Villiers de l'Isle-Adam, wearing the captain's cap of the National Guard, trying to rally the Parnassians to the cause of the Commune. Verlaine, it is true, seemed more excited, more violent to Bergerat. He spoke of chopping off heads and terrified Anatole France by his utterances.

When Thiers ordered civil servants to join the staff at Versailles or at least cease performing their duties, Verlaine ignored this outlandish order. He continued to go to the Hôtel de Ville. One knows little about the duties he performed there. It is generally said that his function was confined to reading the newspapers every day and extracting the most interesting items. Delahaye, however, in whom he confided, assigns him more active functions. Verlaine, he writes, examined the newspapers savagely, designating those that held offending opinions, and gleefully had them suppressed. At first glance this account is credible. But it should be observed that on August 12, 1873, when an account of Verlaine's participation in the Commune was requested, the reply was: unfruitful investigations.

During Bloody Week he witnessed the horrible repression. His mother saw fifty federation men shot down before her eyes, men who, ammunition gone, refused to surrender and shouted: "Capitulators to Sedan!" * He shared the feelings of his friend Blémont and was sickened by the orgy that followed the reestablishment of order and by the cafés crammed with officers and girls. The mourning city, which by day still looked like a cemetery, was little less than a brothel at night.

The group broke up. Cladel took refuge in Montauban. Blémont married. According to Delahaye, a friend employed Verlaine as an insurance broker for a time, but around the

---

* On September 2, 1870, Napoleon III had been defeated and surrendered to the Prussians at Sedan. [Tr.]

month of July the poet became frightened and left for Fampoux with his wife. His cowardice has been made fun of. But Blémont wrote in his diary on June 8 that the civil employees of the Commune were being sought out and that he was worried about his friend. To judge these fears unfounded, one would have to ignore the fact that some days later Verlaine's brother-in-law, Charles de Sivry, was arrested in Néris-les-Bains and taken to Satory where he was imprisoned for several months. His crime was that of having accepted the post of orchestra leader at the Néris casino. This kind of bourgeois justice justified every precaution, excused all fears.

At the end of August, probably on the twenty-third, Verlaine returned with his wife. Danger seemed remote. However, he had lost his job at the Hôtel de Ville. The apartment on Rue du Cardinal-Lemoine was now too heavy an expense, and Verlaine was especially anxious to move to a different section of the city so as to prevent some malicious neighbor from being tempted to denounce him. The Mautés offered their hospitality to the young couple. The second floor of the house was put at the disposal of Mathilde and her husband.

Verlaine renewed his relations with men of letters. After the disaster, the survivors fell in with one another again. Between the men who had shared the anger of the Paris populace and those who had applauded the repression, the gulf was deep. In those times "of intellectual infection," as Verlaine called them, those who had remained uncontaminated banded together: Blémont, Mérat, Cabaner, Valade, the Cros brothers, and with them, Verlaine.

It is all too certain that he had begun to drink again. Lepelletier is positive on this point: his friend had openly resumed his bad habits even before the trip north, right after the end of the Commune. He judges, and doubtless rightly, that by ceasing to work regularly, and by deciding to live in idleness in the home of his wife's parents, Verlaine opened the way for all the misfortunes that followed.

2 · Rimbaud

DURING HIS STAY in Fampoux, such at least is Delahaye's very exact and explicit account, Verlaine had received a letter from Charleville. It was signed by a stranger, Arthur Rimbaud. In this letter the young man described his ideals, his passions, his ennui. He asked for the poet's opinion of the verses he had enclosed with his covering letter. He gave a friend of Verlaine's, Charles Bretagne, as reference; the latter had even written ten lines at the end of the letter in support of young Rimbaud's request. The envelope bore the Rue Nicolet address, so it took some time for it to reach Fampoux. Three days later a second letter came, together with a second parcel of poems.

Verlaine replied from Fampoux—that is, in August, before returning to Paris. He expressed the great interest he had taken in the young stranger's poetry. He let it be understood that it might be possible to help the young man live in Paris, but that he would first have to discuss the matter with his friends. Upon his return to the capital he did, indeed, busy himself with this matter. One day Rimbaud received in Charleville the letter he so longed for; everything was arranged, he was awaited, he could come. A money order, enclosed in the letter, provided him the means of making the trip.

In a very short time an intimacy that brooked no bounds grew up between Verlaine and Rimbaud. They spent their days together on interminable walks around the Butte quarter and later in the cafés of the Trudaine and Latin quarters. They met at the Café de Cluny, at the Tabourey, in a club set up by Verlaine and his friends on the second floor of the Hôtel des Etrangers, on the corner of Rue Racine and Rue de l'Ecole de Médecine. Verlaine came home very late at night, horribly drunk. He no longer bothered about his linen and had adopted Rimbaud's slovenly style of dress. Soon, people in literary circles began to gossip. On November 16, one newspaper noted that among the personalities seen at a dramatic performance was Monsieur Paul Verlaine "with a charming young thing, Mademoiselle Rimbaud, on his arm." The thrust seems cruel; but it was if anything an understatement. In reality, the two men had strolled around the lounge of the theater with their arms around each other's necks!

One incident succeeded in alienating the admiration that Rimbaud's verses had first won him. Verlaine and his friends had again taken up a prewar custom—the Vilains Bonshommes (the Bad Goodfellows)—dinners. They met every month over a wineseller's shop at the corner of Rue Bonaparte and Place Saint-Sulpice. One day, Rimbaud, in a rather excited state, interrupted an obscure rhymester who was reciting some ridiculous verses, then attacked Carjat with Verlaine's sword stick. He was easily disarmed. However, they decided that from then on the author of *Fêtes galantes* (Love's Revels) would be invited alone and without his companion. Ruffled by this ostracism, Verlaine broke with the Vilains Bonshommes, that is, in effect, with his whole group of friends.

One may guess what home life on Rue Nicolet had become. Mathilde was pregnant but her husband had neither attention nor respect for her condition. One day she ventured to observe that Rimbaud was not altogether nice: Verlaine pulled her out of bed and threw her on the floor. On October 30, she gave birth to a boy. Verlaine had not been home all day. He did not come in until midnight. He seemed pleased, kissed his wife and the baby. Everything went well for three days. He began to have dinner at home again and spent his evenings with Mathilde. But on the fourth day, he came home drunk and broke into such violence that the nurse wanted to call for help. He showed no affection for the young mother and child. On the fifteenth, he repeated the scene of November 4. Monsieur Mauté was obliged to intervene to protect his daughter. From that time on, late homecomings with their violent accompaniments were the rule.

By the beginning of January 1872, scenes had become an everyday occurrence. On the thirteenth, Verlaine nearly strangled Mathilde. The poor woman's neck was covered with contusions. The doctor was called in. Verlaine promised to apologize. But the next day he refused, made another scene that evening and left to sleep elsewhere, perhaps at his mother's. Then Mathilde decided to leave. With her child, she took refuge in Périgueux. When Verlaine, calmed down, returned to Rue Nicolet, he was refused entry and was told that his wife was no longer in Paris. He did not know where she was.

One must believe that in spite of his violent actions he had never expected this separation. He implored. On January 20 he sent a letter to Mathilde, to the Rue Nicolet address, acknowledging and regretting his behavior; this letter was one day to serve the Mautés in court as supporting evidence for their charges against their son-in-law. For the time being they insisted on Rimbaud's departure. Verlaine could not make up his mind to it. So the elder Mauté had recourse to more forcible means. Through a summons Verlaine was advised that his wife was filing a request for separation on the grounds of the assault, brutality, and injuries of which her husband was guilty. The presiding judge, however, granted a series of postponements that allowed time for matters to be straightened out. Verlaine spoke later of that "fateful month of February" in which he managed, by his repentant behavior, to give proof of the affection he still had for his wife. Insofar as it is possible to establish definite chronology, Rimbaud went back to Charleville during the first half of March.

Such are the known facts. One should like to know more and be able to give a full account of those months of frenzy and passion, to determine the role played therein by Rimbaud, to discover at the bottom of all this degradation what, if any, spiritual life might subsist. From an examination of Verlaine's actions and behavior alone, it is clear that this crisis of 1871–1872 is a renewal of that of 1869. Verlaine is behaving toward Mathilde just as he had behaved two years earlier toward his mother. The same homicidal rages provoked or abetted by

drunkenness. The same outbursts of wild frenzy in this custo-
marily gentle, affectionate, well-behaved man, when he loses
consciousness and gives himself over to his demons. Morbid
states of mind that fall into the province of psychiatry are evident here.

This is meant to imply that it is not perhaps satisfactory to
explain the whole matter by the presence of Rimbaud. A number of historians have felt obliged to discover and establish the
degree of responsibility of each man. For some, it is Rimbaud
who corrupted Verlaine. Others, on the contrary, maintain that
Verlaine ruined the young man from Ardennes. Absurd simpli-
fication! Who can believe that in 1871 Mathilde's husband had
yet to be corrupted? And who imagine that young Rimbaud—
in a constant state of crisis since the beginning of the year—
brought his innocence to Paris with him? Setting aside all oversimple explanations, however, it still seems clear that despite
their difference in age, Verlaine was the pupil and studied under
his diabolical companion. Up to that point he had been a weak
man, yet it was not without remorse that he gave in to his vices.
Rimbaud made him, for a time at least, an "offspring of the
sun." He coldly urged him to deny all discipline, to defy moral
laws, and to loathe responsibility. He taught him to be ashamed
of his remorse, he reproached him for what he called his weaknesses: and of all things, was not the most shameful weakness,
in his eyes, Verlaine's compassion for, and the persistence with
which he loved, Mathilde and his child? It was not Rimbaud
who made Verlaine a wild and brutal drunk. But he found it
amusing to set loose in his friend those demoniacal forces he
had been delighted to discover in the author of *La Bonne
Chanson.*

Cruel aberration, for which both Rimbaud and Verlaine
would one day blush. It should be understood, however, that
it was not simply, as certain biographers would have it, an
ignoble entanglement. In his madness, Rimbaud was pursuing
the discovery of a "new love." He dreamed of a humanity that
would be truly free, heroical, and happy. He opened up these
vistas before the dazzled Verlaine. The latter, for the past year,
had had the sensation that he was sinking into the mediocrity
of middle-class contentment. He had perceived its shabbiness,

the hypocritical sham of it. He was acquainted as well with all the false intellectuality of literary milieus, that spectacle of literature and art that masked self-seeking and financial interest. He felt suffocated. He recognized that his young companion was revealing to him at last values that were genuine. We know well enough that the most elevated significance of this message escaped him, that Elisa Dehée's spoiled child was incapable of embracing in all its breadth the revelation Rimbaud made to him. But his joy, his exaltation, his belief that he was escaping being swallowed up are not the less authentic and give his relations with the young man their real significance. Moreover, Rimbaud was not only a satanic teacher but a child of marvelous sensitivities, with qualities of artlessness and freshness, and the affecting frailties of a woman. If one insists on disregarding these bases of a dreadful entanglement, one closes the door to understanding certain of Verlaine's poems, and these among the most beautiful utterances the tragic sense of life has ever wrenched from man.

Around March 15 Mathilde came back. Verlaine evinced great joy, and the young woman had reason to believe that peace had returned. He had found a job with the Belgian branch of Lloyd's. That evening he went out with her. A new friend occupied his attention, young Forain, whom he called "the little dark-haired darling." Mathilde saw no harm in this. Forain did not drink. He showed himself to be pleasant, cheerful, likeable. Thanks to his good influence, Verlaine did not get drunk.

Alas, Verlaine was not acting in good faith. He was secretly arranging for the return of "the blond darling"—Rimbaud. The latter was in correspondence with him. His letters were sent to Verlaine's mother's address when they were confined to complaints about their separation. They were sent to Forain's address when they spoke of his imminent return. It was a question of waiting for a little while, of being patient for a few weeks until such time as the Verlaine household should be "all patched up." They had, moreover, decided to be more discreet, and Rimbaud promised to be "less frightful in appearance." As Verlaine said in his elliptical style: "linen, shine, comb, the niceties." They planned requitals, "tigerish" things, to punish those responsible for their separation.

In May Rimbaud came back to Paris. On the eighteenth, it is said. But a new quarrel had already broken out at Rue Nicolet on the ninth: Mathilde had come out of her room that morning with a split lip and a lump on her forehead. In June she noticed that her husband was limping. He had several wounds on his thigh. She was one day to learn that Rimbaud had come back and that he and Verlaine played at fighting with knives. On June 15 a terrible scene took place. Verlaine went after Mathilde, weapon in hand. She took refuge at her father's side. Verlaine raised his stick at the old man. The latter, still vigorous, was able to knock him down and disarm him.

THE FLIGHT

The sixth of July passed in peace. The following day Mathilde was ill with neuralgia and a bit of fever. Verlaine seemed concerned. He told her that he would stop by Dr. Cros's on his way to the office. He left after kissing her affectionately. If one may trust the account he gave later, he chanced to meet Rimbaud who informed him that he was going back to Charleville; Verlaine begged him not to leave him alone again, and when the young man stubbornly persisted, he is supposed to have said: "All right, I'm going with you." This is the traditional version. There is good reason to suspect that this departure was, on the contrary, anticipated and planned. It has even been said that Verlaine's mother, who was very much provoked against the Mautés, had been informed and had furnished the necessary money for the trip. As for Mathilde, she noted that her husband had seemed sad and was very affectionate when he left her.

When Verlaine took the train in Rimbaud's company he was not thinking of leaving France. He was simply going to Fampoux to visit his relatives, and one may well believe that he had no notion of breaking definitively with Mathilde. Delahaye is the only one who makes this assertion, and he is right. He adds that Verlaine had just had a sudden fright because a reactionary newspaper had published his name as one of the writers involved in the events of the Commune. That is why Verlaine and Rimbaud took the train, not from the Gare de l'Est but from the Gare du Nord, and not for Charleville but for Arras.

Having arrived in that town, they went to eat in a café. They attracted attention by their incendiary remarks. The police stepped in and made them go back to Paris. Delahaye claims that then Verlaine became frightened and decided that it was no longer safe for him in France. Once back at the Gare du Nord the two travelers went directly to the Gare de l'Est and this time reached Charleville. They crossed the Belgian border at night and arrived in Brussels by way of Walcourt and Charleroi.

In that city Verlaine decided to send news of himself to his wife and his mother. To the latter he wrote: "Always write me in two separate parts, one that can be shown to Rimbaud, the other about my poor household." He sent his address, the Hôtel Liégeois, to Mathilde. Dauntless, she came running. Her mother accompanied her. This was on July 21.

Mathilde had written Verlaine and had arranged to meet him at the Hôtel Liégeois. She got off the train at five in the morning. Verlaine was not at the hotel. He came in at eight o'clock. The account of this meeting has been oversimplified through reliance on the poems in his "Birds in the Night." It is possible that Mathilde behaved very affectionately and that she managed to revive her husband's sensual ardor. But several accounts agree in saying that matters went otherwise. Verlaine began by declaring that they no longer belonged to one another, that reconciliation was impossible, and that it was too late. "Home life is hateful to me," he kept repeating. He spoke quite openly of his love for Rimbaud. "We love like tigers," he is supposed to have said. He is even supposed to have shown her his chest lacerated with knife cuts. Mathilde listened without comprehending. She misinterpreted the meaning of these confessions, which she was not to appreciate until later. She begged her husband to return with her. One credible version has it that Verlaine then proposed that she accept his friendship with Rimbaud in a kind of *ménage à trois*. She refused, but proposed that he and she take a trip. He refused in turn. Then he agreed to think it over until evening.

They met again at five o'clock in a public garden near the Gare du Midi, and there Mathilde drew out of Verlaine a mumbled and barely audible semblance of consent. Her mother stood by a few steps away. The three of them got on the train. Judging from the route they took, they intended to go first to Fampoux. At the border station of Quiévrain, they got off for customs. When it was time to go back to their compartment, Verlaine refused to get aboard. "No, I'm staying!" he declared, jamming his felt hat on his head with a punch. Mathilde was never to see him again.

The two men stayed in Brussels for six weeks, and no one knows anything definite about what they did there. Verlaine merely says that they did "a little of everything." They took little care to hide the nature of their relations and a police report says bluntly: "The two lovers have been seen in Brussels, openly practicing their love."

LONDON

According to Delahaye, it was lack of resources that made the two Frenchmen decide to leave Belgium and seek their fortune in London. On September 7, they embarked from Ostend on the Dover mailboat. They arrived in London the next day, which was a Sunday. There they rented a room at 34–35 Howland Street, Fitzroy Square, in a high-windowed eighteenth century building, once elegant but now run-down. Its French proprietor rented out rooms to tailors, artists, and a few bohemians from among his compatriots.

In London Verlaine found a good number of his old friends— Régamey, Andrieu, Lissagaray, Vermersch. He joined the Social Studies Circle that Lissagaray had founded and that brought together the "frock-coated men" of the Commune. We have important information about his appearance at this time. He had few clothes but dressed well enough, was cheerful, and not at all cast down by his fate. Hours spent with him were delightful hours. He had a silent companion, Rimbaud, in tow.

But this cheerfulness, this pleasantness, concealed a deep anxiety. In Paris almost all of Verlaine's friends were taking his wife's side. Even Pelletan and D'Hervilly were turning against him. Valade, Forain, the Cros brothers, and, he believed, Burty, alone remained faithful to him. And above all, the Mautés had filed a request for separation. Not long after the flight in July, they had found Rimbaud's letters among their son-in-law's papers. They had been enlightened as to the real nature of his relations with Verlaine. They had become aware that they had been deceived about the March reconciliation. This time they had decided to free their daughter legally from any obligation to her unworthy husband. Maître Guyot-Sionnest, their lawyer, was pursuing the matter vigorously. Verlaine was obliged to retain a lawyer himself. On the advice of a friend of the family, an old pettifogger named Istace, he chose Maître Pérard, a lawyer on Rue du Quatre-Septembre.

Toward the end of November 1872, Rimbaud decided to go back to Charleville. Some have thought that he was weary of the poverty of their life, which assumes that the two men were living like beggars; the error is obvious, for Verlaine's mother, if it had been necessary, would have sent the needed money. Actually, it was Rimbaud's mother who made her son understand that, in the interests of all concerned, he should return to France, and that his departure would deprive the Mautés of the strongest evidence for their charges against Verlaine. Verlaine's mother probably lent her support to this wise advice; perhaps Mathilde, finally heartened, would consent to be reconciled with her husband.

Thus Verlaine stayed on alone in London in an isolation that soon became unendurable to him. At the beginning of January 1873 he fell ill. He summoned his mother and his wife by telegram. Only the former answered his appeal. Two days later, Rimbaud arrived; the elderly Elisa had alerted him and had sent him the fifty francs needed for the trip. Then, early in February, Madame Verlaine left, and although the contrary has long been believed, Rimbaud stayed. His British Museum reading card has been found. It is dated March 25, 1873.

If one were better informed about Verlaine's and Rimbaud's conduct and thoughts during the early months of 1873, one might perhaps discover something quite different from the constructions that have been put upon them. One persistent rumor in the Verlaine family, which may pertain to a number of unpublished documents, has it that Madame Verlaine, at her sick son's bedside, opened his eyes to his follies, and that he was deeply affected by her maternal reproofs. One thing is certain, that from that time on he thought of nothing but rein-

gratiating himself with Mathilde. He prepared to return. At
one point he contemplated returning to Paris and went to
Newhaven to board a ship headed for Dieppe. But he became
frightened because he believed that the French police were on
the lookout for him. Fancy perhaps; but we now know that a
police informant in London never ceased to follow his slightest
movements and made reports on him as one might on a dangerous criminal.

Thus Verlaine decided to rejoin his friends and family in
Belgium. On April 4, with Rimbaud, he boarded the "Comtesse
de Flandre." On arrival the two men separated; Rimbaud went
to Roche, where he arrived on April 11, and Verlaine went to
Namur. He called on Canon Lambin, a friend of the Grand-
jeans, and on the two Delogne brothers, priests who had been
rectors of Paliseul and who held high-ranking posts in the
diocese. He asked them to intercede with Mathilde. They
could only, alas, offer him consoling words, and almost immediately a letter arrived from his wife that removed all hope of
reconciliation. It was a terrible blow. He fell ill and spoke of a
"cerebral stroke" that nearly killed him. Verlaine doubtless
remained obsessed by the thought of Rimbaud, and the desire
he showed for a reconciliation with Mathilde was only play-
acting. But even if dissimulation played a large part, it is likely
that he sincerely wished to regain his home. Perhaps he had
an even more pressing reason for making up with his wife. He
had been informed, he claimed, that she was on the point of
giving in to the urgent attentions of a friend. He feared that
the situation would become irreparable before he had a chance
to make amends for his madness of the preceding July.

He went to live in Jehonville at his Aunt Evrard's. He followed the course of his case from there. On October 13, 1872,
the presiding judge had issued a *pendente lite* decree, authoriz-
ing Mathilde's continued residence with her parents and assign-
ing the child to her. The Mautés now actively pressed the
action for separation from bed and board. Verlaine, meanwhile,
continued to correspond with Rimbaud and even saw him now
and then. When it became obvious that the Mautés would be
intractable, Mathilde's husband prepared to return to London
with his companion. On May 19 he announced that he would

leave in a week. Indeed, on May 25, he met Rimbaud in Bouillon, and they started out for Antwerp. They sailed on May 27. On arriving in London the following day they took lodgings at 8 Great College, Camden Town.

This second stay was to last until July 10. It appears that this time they were short of funds and the two friends experienced, if not actual poverty, at least discomfort. They lived by giving a few private lessons. Four "want ads" have been found in English newspapers in which two French gentlemen offer to give lessons for whose perfection, quality, and moderate price they freely vouch. The result was but middling. Verlaine claimed that in the end they managed to make from 100 to 150 francs a month. But if one is to trust Rimbaud's account, they succeeded in amassing no more than a dozen francs a week. It is perhaps this state of affairs that explains why Verlaine again took flight.

BRUSSELS

The traditional version—just as for the events of July 1872—emphasizes the unexpected, the spontaneous character of this action. But Edmond Lepelletier maintains that, on the contrary, Verlaine had planned this flight in accord with and on the advice of his mother. His account is convincing: a number of details seem to confirm it in positive fashion.

Whatever Verlaine's intentions may have been, a quarrel broke out between him and Rimbaud on the morning of July 3. From a collation of the evidence, it appears that Rimbaud had criticized him for his laziness, and that he took it very badly. It is also possible that Rimbaud had asked him for money, and that his refusal provoked the quarrel. He decided to take the first boat for Antwerp. He left very hastily, leaving behind his clothes, his books, and his manuscripts. Did he tell Rimbaud he was leaving? At any rate, the latter met him at the dock and urged him in vain to stay on. On July 4, in Brussels, Verlaine took a room at the Hôtel Liégeois and wrote to his mother. She came immediately.

He also wrote to Mathilde. He declared in his letter that he was leaving Rimbaud forever, that he had left him alone in London, and that he would kill himself if his wife did not immediately come to join him in Brussels. But Mathilde threw this letter into a drawer without ever opening it. Five years were to pass before she would know the distracted message it contained.

It is easy to make fun of these ineffectual threats of suicide. They are nonetheless an expression of genuine despair. Verlaine never really wanted the mess. Even when he left France with Rimbaud, he neither wanted nor anticipated a break with his wife. He had been playing hooky. He was acting as children do. But at this point he perceived the hopeless nature of the situation he had got himself into: his home destroyed, his poetic ambitions rendered unattainable, his fortune wasted, and only loneliness and poverty to look forward to.

When at the end of a few days it was clear that his wife was not going to respond to his call, he decided to give some sign to Rimbaud. The latter had been in despair. He begged Verlaine to rejoin him, he promised to be good, he assured him of his love. Finally on July 8, a Tuesday, Verlaine sent him a telegram: "Come here, Hôtel Liégeois," it read. Rimbaud was probably en route at that very moment, for he arrived in Brussels that forenoon. The two men and Madame Verlaine went to stay at the Hôtel de Courtrai, 1 Rue des Brasseurs.

No one knows what they did on the day of the ninth. But that evening Verlaine was drunk. On Tuesday, July 10, he went out early. He started drinking again. No one knows what was going on in his mind, but he bought a revolver. He returned to the hotel at noon. He was still drunk. He showed Rimbaud the weapon he had just bought: "It's for you, me, everybody," he declared. Then the two men went out together, had a drink, and ate together. They came back. They had been quarreling all the while. Rimbaud persisted in saying that he was going back to France. Verlaine kept repeating that if he tried to leave something awful would happen. In the end, Verlaine locked the door to the room, sat down facing Rimbaud, and loaded his revolver. Rimbaud was standing in front of him, his right shoulder leaning against the wall. Verlaine fired twice. The first shot hit Rimbaud in the left forearm. The second bullet struck the wall about a foot above the ground. Madame Verlaine, who was in the adjoining room, rushed in. She found her son in tears, begging Rimbaud to put a bullet through his head.

Then things calmed down. They went to Saint-Jean hospital where Rimbaud's arm was dressed. They began to talk things over reasonably. Rimbaud announced that he was leaving. Verlaine and his mother decided to accompany him to the Gare du Midi. But on the way the dispute flared up again. Near the Place Rouppe Verlaine made a move, planting himself in front of Rimbaud and barring his way. Did he stop at putting his hand in his pocket? Delahaye says that he pulled out his revolver. From the very muddled account of everybody from Verlaine to Byvanck, it is clear at least that Verlaine once again threatened his companion. Rimbaud, frightened, turned tail, and sought the protection of a policeman. The latter took the two men to the police station. Questions were asked. They had difficulty answering them. An hour later Verlaine was locked up.

3 · Redress

BELGIAN JUSTICE was inexorable. First of all, because the examining magistrate had seized letters that left little doubt as to the relations between the two Frenchmen, suspicions which were confirmed by medical examination. But also because the magistrate saw Verlaine as a former supporter of the Commune, a dangerous fellow under surveillance by various police agencies, from whom middle-class society should be protected. On July 11, he was transferred, handcuffed, in a police van, to the Petits-Carmes prison. That day he underwent his first interrogation. On the fifteenth, medicolegal examination. On the eighteenth, a second interrogation. On the nineteenth, and too late, Rimbaud withdrew all action and waived all charges. The inquiry proceeded. The lack of validity of the initial charges became apparent. Impossible to establish premeditation and criminal intent. Assault and battery causing unfitness for work was established. On August 8 Verlaine appeared before the sixth chamber of the court of summary jurisdiction. He was sentenced to a maximum of two years in jail. He appealed. On August 27 the sentence was upheld. He was kept in the Petits-Carmes for two more months. Then on October 25 he was taken to the Mons prison. It was there that he was to work out the rest of his penalty.

It is Verlaine's own fault that these eighteen months of imprisonment have often been described in almost cheerful terms. During his last years, in Paris, we may easily see how prison life —monotonous, but orderly and free of anxiety—should have

seemed to him more agreeable than the horrible existence he
was then leading. Moreover, the legend that he was in the
process of constructing around his name required that the period
of his conversion should also be a period of contented peace and
quiet. But the letters he wrote from Mons strike quite a different note. He had already suffered from dreadful headaches in
Brussels. In November 1873 the courage he had maintained up
to that point seemed to leave him. He spent his days sorting
coffee beans. This life of isolation, as opposed to mere loneliness,
these hours filled by prison duties, extinguished the activity of
his mind, made any serious work impossible. He was for a long
time unable to write verse. Perhaps, however, these conditions
improved toward the end. He was able to read, study English,
and return to studying the Spanish he had let drop for the last
ten years. The prison warden was good to him, and the chaplain, Father Eugène Descamps, who had undoubtedly received
letters from Namur and Paliseul, hoped more keenly than anyone for the prisoner's conversion.

His stay in Mons was marked by one important event. He
was converted. In the strict sense of the word. Verlaine pros-
trated himself before the crucifix. He accepted Catholic dogma
with all his soul, he received the sacraments, he scrupulously
observed the obligations of Christian life. One should also take
into account the actual context of this conversion, which was
equally a return: a return to the beliefs and practices of his
youth.

According to Verlaine's account, he lost his faith the year following his First Communion. But we have noted above facts
that contradict or modify this statement: that he made confession as late as 1869, and that he attended lectures at Notre-
Dame for a number of years. Le Fefve de Vivy's studies have
shown how strong and enduring a hold religious training had
on the young Parisian boy, and how quickly it regained its
strength as soon as he once again came under the pure and
Christian influence of the paternal household. He was probably more truly estranged from the Church around 1867–1869
when he was associating with the young Parnassians, almost all
of whom were anticlerical and atheistic. Joining his voice to
theirs, he had written a sonnet in which he defied heaven and

ancient superstition. His letters from London, in 1872, show
that he had taken up Rimbaud's habit of using certain blasphemous turns of phrase. But on this point as well as on others we
should not give these attitudes total credence. Certainly the
Verlaine who posed as a blasphemous swaggerer before his
Paris associates bore no resemblance to the Verlaine of Jehonville and Paliseul. However, that Verlaine was not the less real,
nor perhaps the less sincere. It is a matter here of the fitfulness
of attitudes and words of one of the most changeable and torn
of men.

He had been drawing close to the Church since January 1873.
Le Fefve de Vivy apparently has good sources when he writes
that Verlaine had at that time "informed" the Fathers Delogne
and Canon Lambin of Namur "of his conversion." He reports
that in May 1873 at Jehonville Verlaine had promised the priest
to return to the Church. His account sheds light on one of
Delahaye's anecdotes, which has it that one day in the spring
of the same year Verlaine spoke of the sudden veerings of the
human soul. The conversation took place in Bouillon: the
persons with whom he was conversing were Rimbaud and
Delahaye. Verlaine told how a few years earlier he had one day
gone into a church, how, impelled by an unknown force, he
had entered the confession box, and that he had then, for a
period of one or two weeks, begun again to practice Catholicism. Rimbaud listened to these confidences soberly and without
one word of irony.

Seen in this perspective, the conversion of 1874 does not
seem less genuine, but its character is clearer. It is not true that
Verlaine had for many years broken off all contact with the
Church. Quite the reverse of godless, he was, rather, a weak
Christian gone wrong. His conversion is essentially a return
to beliefs and practices abandoned but a short time before,
beliefs and practices that had never completely lost their attrac-
tion.

That doubtless explains why, in November of 1873, Verlaine
was composing "some Canticles to Mary and some Early
Church prayers," whereas the actual conversion did not take
place until the following May. We may be certain that Verlaine
wrote these poems of Christian inspiration in complete sin-

cerity; and not because he was about to become a Christian again, but because in his own way he already was one, and always had been one. It is enough for him to find himself removed from both the Parnassian group and Rimbaud for his still close past and his religious feeling, which had never been entirely stifled, to regain force and inspire him. Not to mention that in his new surroundings everything conspired to lead him in that direction. The prison schedule included prayer and attendance at Mass. Father Descamps kept watch over him and awaited the propitious moment.

This moment came in the spring of 1874. On April 24, the Seine tribunal delivered judgment of separation of bed and board between Mathilde and the Mons prison inmate. Jurisdiction over little Georges was awarded to the mother. When he learned this news, Verlaine broke down. He had the chaplain called. He received from him books of religious instruction. In June, he announced his conversion to the priest. A short time after, he made confession and received Communion.

It is doubtless somewhat unrewarding to comment further on an action so anticipated and, one might readily add, so natural. What should be noted rather is the dual nature of Verlaine's Catholicism. The surprising thing about his conversion was the way this unhappy and blameworthy man went immediately, directly, and quite spontaneously, to the core of the Christian spirit. He embraced the doctrine of the Fall and Redemption. He was the sinner who in the depths of his abjection raises his prayer to Christ Who redeems and cleanses. Later his religious feeling was expressed in more scholastic terms, hardened into a sometimes unpleasant dogmatism. But during these first years, it was admirable in its strength, richness, and authenticity.

At the same time, however, it meant for Verlaine a break with the modern world. From that time on, and until his death, there was to be in him a prophet inveighing against this "abominable, rotten, vile, stupid, proud, and damned" society. Nothing would escape his denunciations, neither democracy, the Republic, universal suffrage, Victor Hugo, Flaubert, nor the Goncourt brothers. Previously, when he was an Hébertist partisan, he would willingly have lopped off heads. Now he would burn people at the stake. It is the same fanaticism. His favorite newspaper is *L'Univers,* and his intellectual master, Joseph de Maistre. The Oratorians, Montalembert, and Monsignor Dupanloup are bad Catholics in the eyes of this new convert. In his zeal he confuses the cause of the Church—"which has made France"—and that of the Legitimist party.

All this orthodox fervor was not enough to fool anyone. The prison authorities judged him astutely. They noted his weak character and described his moral conduct as only "fairly good." They were disturbed at not finding in him any inclination to work. They considered his reform only "likely." Steps had been taken in Brussels to have his sentence commuted. They were unavailing. It was only through the strictest application of the provisions of the regulations that Verlaine obtained a remission of 169 days. He was released from prison on January 16, 1875.

STICKNEY AND BOURNEMOUTH

His mother was at the gate waiting for him. She took him to Fampoux. In prison he had dreamed of taking up some kind of farming. But his reception by the family was reserved. Lepelletier tells us so, and Mathilde lends further veracity to his account in relating that Victorine Dehée had taken her side and gave her news of Verlaine's plans. The latter still dreamed of a reconciliation with his wife. He went to Paris and was quickly convinced that he had nothing to hope for. It is possible that he considered becoming a Trappist monk. A week's retreat at the monastery of La Trappe de Chimay made him realize his mistake. Finally he undertook to convert Rimbaud. He decided to go to Stuttgart to find him and win him over. He found a Rimbaud who was barely recognizable—proper, a rummager in libraries, and concerned only with learning German. We know little about the way in which the meeting ended. People have spoken of a walk outside the city, of blows exchanged; it has been said that some peasants found Verlaine unconscious in a ditch and that he stayed in bed at their home for several days. But this account is at variance with one of Rimbaud's letters: "Verlaine stayed two and a half days and, at my urging, returned to Paris, in order to go and finish his studies *over there on the island* right away."

It is with this last part that Verlaine's movements tally. He arrived in London around March 20, 1875. He took lodgings at 10 London Street, Fitzroy Square, right next to Howland Street. But he had no intention of lingering there. He applied to an agency for a job. In a few days' time he received notice that there was a job for him at Stickney, in Lincolnshire, about eight miles from Boston and about 125 miles north of London. He went there on March 31.

Twenty years later he set down his recollections of the twelve months he spent there. One may guess what inaccuracies have crept into his account. Some close investigations have rectified these. He left behind him in that peaceful village of eight hundred inhabitants the memory of a gentle, patient, and rather sad man. He attended Anglican Sunday services, but on Saturday he rose very early to attend Catholic Mass in Boston. He spent his free time in reading and taking long walks. His conduct, witnesses say, was irreproachable. With the exception of one person who saw him one day, on the way back from Boston, "most gloriously tipt," everyone agrees in saying that he did not drink. The rector, Reverend Coltman, and W. Andrews, the young director of the school, esteemed him, and his students liked him.

He was not unhappy. For the first time in his life he knew calm, silence, and solitude with freedom. He had news from Paris only from time to time, and for the time being had no wish to return to that city which for him was bound up with terrible memories. A few rare friends continued to correspond with him. Delahaye kept him up to date on Rimbaud's travels and even passed on to him some of his old companion's letters. These have been lost. We possess one of Verlaine's replies. Its lack of warmth and its wily and preachy self-righteousness leave a heart-rending impression. On the other hand, he had formed a friendship, in April 1875, with Germain Nouveau, who had been Rimbaud's companion a year earlier and whom he had the pleasure of leading back to the Christian faith.

He had not renounced all ambition. He needed to restore his fortune, which had been drastically reduced by his recent follies, and his job at Stickney was too poorly paid. In October he had already begun to think of leaving as soon as he could

find a better post. The six-month contract he had signed ran
out in the middle or toward the end of November. Mr. Andrews
persuaded him to stay until Christmas by promising more ad-
vantageous terms. Then he agreed a second time to prolong
his stay. But he was looking elsewhere. He thought he had found
something. He was led to believe that he might live in Boston
by setting up courses or by tutoring. Therefore, around April
1, he left his Stickney friends. But his disillusionment in Boston
was great. Only three pupils showed up. He had once again to
look for something else.

On June 1, 1876, he left Boston and went to spend a few
weeks in London. He was counting on finding a post for the
following school year. He also went to France—and may even
have gone to Paliseul, for Delahaye saw him in Charleville.
His health was perfect at the time, and his friend was struck
by his changed appearance—his vigorous and lithe body, his
lively step, and his fresh and delightful good spirits.

In September he started work at St.-Aloysius Institute in
Bournemouth. The owner-director's name was Frederick Rem-
ington, but the name of the establishment is indication enough
that the Jesuits had the upper hand there. The atmosphere was
quite unlike that of Stickney. Bournemouth is a fashionable
town on the southern coast of England. St.-Aloysius Institute
was small but very "select," and the boarding fees were high.
The director showed little interest in either the behavior or the
studies of the young sluggards of good family entrusted to his
care. Verlaine was to suffer from their lack of discipline.

He had got into the habit during the last two years of spending his vacations in France. When he went to Paris, he stayed
with his friend Istace, who ran a cabaret at 12 Rue de Lyon.
More frequently, and for longer periods, he stayed at his
mother's house in Arras. Madame Verlaine had settled there,
at 2 Impasse d'Elbronne, Rue d'Amiens. Delahaye went there
to spend a few days with his friend. He described the house
as well lit and tidy, the old armchairs in speckled velvet, and
Madame Verlaine as bustling, slender, quick, and very much
occupied in preparing delicate dishes for her son and his visitor.
Verlaine's vacation companions were Delahaye and Irénée

Decroix. They took happy walks together in the environs of Arras and as far as Saint-Pol.

Verlaine began to miss Paris. In January 1877 he was already thinking of returning to France, this time for good. He anticipated that this would be at Easter. From an examination of the inadequate number of records available, he seems to have left Bournemouth in April but to have returned there a little later, around June, doubtless to supervise the students staying in boarding school during vacation. He left the institute for good around the middle of September.

RETHEL

He went to Paris. He had no definite plans. At the time he was still inclined to return to England and try his luck in another English school. But he was also looking for something in the way of nonstate education in France. His friend Delahaye, indeed, had just left the post he occupied at the Institution Notre-Dame in Rethel. Verlaine, without telling him, applied for the job and got it. He was appointed assistant to a certain Monsieur Eugène Royer, who conducted "vocational courses preparing for the Ecoles d'Arts et Métiers, and for government and military service examinations." In plain terms, and all bluffing aside, he taught French, English, and history to the "Latinless" divisions, as they were then scornfully designated. Verlaine was made responsible for thirty hours of classes a week.

He filled this post for two years, from October 1877 to June 1879. He gave the head of the establishment cause for satisfaction. He seemed happy in this new milieu whose religious beliefs and political sympathies he shared. He was spoken of as a good teacher, reliable, competent, and reserved. Perhaps even a little too solemn. The recollections of one of his former pupils give us a number of rather piquant details on this subject. Enveloped in a long and threadbare frock coat, he walked with the stiff gait of an automaton. His face had a rapt expression. He appeared to be immersed in endless meditation. He kept his arms crossed on his chest, his hands spread out. The ecclesiastical staff thought this layman was overdoing it, and the students, with their lively sense of the ridiculous, called him Jesus Christ.

They laughed at his ostentation in serving at Mass. He took Communion every Sunday.

Unfortunately he began to drink again. According to certain *Souvenirs,* he went into town after his morning classes and had long stints at Père Martin's winery. More than once, they say, he was unable to make it back to school; so often that his superiors were obliged to schedule all his classes in the morning. Verlaine gave quite a different version of the facts to Cazals. Having come back a little tipsy once or twice, he was reprimanded and promised not to do it again. He kept his promise for several months. But one evening he came back completely drunk and took the reproaches made him very badly. He was fired. Some biographers have said that, to lend an appearance of politeness to their decision, Verlaine's superiors informed him that to their regret the post he occupied had been dropped. But it is evident from one of Delahaye's letters, written at that very time, that another tack was taken. They offered Verlaine less satisfactory terms, which he had the good taste to turn down.

LUCIEN LÉTINOIS

In the preceding months he had formed a very lively friendship with one of his pupils, Lucien Létinois. He was a young peasant of nineteen. He was tall and thin, with regular features, lively eyes, a countenance which, Delahaye reports, radiated good will and vigor. It is true that Lepelletier, who liked him little, wrote that he looked like a roughhewn and conceited bumpkin. But a letter quoted by Marcel Coulon says that on the contrary: "Lucien was likeable, lively, boyish." Verlaine became attached to him. He called him his son. When he had to leave the school at Rethel, Lucien had just failed his diploma exams. His studies were at an end. Verlaine conceived the plan of going to England with his pupil. The young man's parents gave their approval.

Verlaine and Lucien arrived in England at the end of August 1879. They went first to Stickney, where Verlaine set the young man up in the post he had himself filled four years earlier. He left him there and went to Lymington where he had found a job for himself. In this little port town, facing the Isle of

Wight, Mr. William Murdoch conducted the Solent Collegiate School. Verlaine was in charge of French classes. But all his attention was fixed on young Lucien who, far away from him, was trying his hand at teaching and succeeding very badly.

On Christmas Eve 1879, the two Frenchmen met in London. They intended to spend the Christmas holidays together. The fog was thick. Verlaine found his "son" sad and troubled. He questioned him and received his confession of a lapse, the nature of which is not too difficult to guess. In the strictness of his moral principles, and also perhaps because Lucien's confession touched off in him a feeling less innocent than he knew, Verlaine went into a panic. He immediately sent the young man to confession. Then, abandoning England and their jobs at Stickney and Lymington, the men went back to France.

Biographers have contrived to make this episode, of which Verlaine gives an account in a poem in *Amour*, seem a dismal and unsavory affair. One must say, and say again, that their account is based on a misinterpretation. The only evidence they have is poem VIII of *Amour*, and one has only to read it in conjunction with other parts of Verlaine's testimony, to see how mistaken they are, to understand that the "mortal sin" the poet speaks of has no reference to a diabolical connection between teacher and pupil, but quite simply to Lucien's weakness in allowing himself to be beguiled by the charms of a young Stickney miss.

Having returned to France in the last days of 1879, Verlaine resolved to live with Lucien on a farm that they would cultivate together. This plan may seem mad. But we should not jump to conclusions. Verlaine had already envisaged this solution on leaving prison, and there is reason to believe that his mother encouraged him in this direction. Thus, he bought a piece of property in Juniville, south of Rethel, and settled there with Lucien. The young man's parents, who occupied a plot of land a few miles away in the village of Coulommes, left it to come to live with their son. They moved in at the beginning of March 1880.

Verlaine thought he had finally found "the little corner, the little niche" where he might end his days in peace. Only Germain Nouveau, Istace, and Lepelletier knew his new address.

He concealed it from everyone else, and the few friends he retained sent their letters to Fampoux, to the Dehées, who forwarded them. One reliable source has described him at this period. His conversation was very enjoyable. He spoke in a monotone, with few gestures, his language unassuming. What he had to say was not sprightly but very interesting. It is true that the villagers were amazed by him. Gossipy tongues wagged over the life spent together by a man of thirty-six and a boy of twenty. But historians are not obliged to share in the opinions of dolts.

Unfortunately the enterprise went badly and debts accumulated. It has been said that Verlaine did not work and hindered the other's work. This may readily be believed. But it has been said, too, that the elder Létinois wanted to make a killing with the property that had been purchased in his name, and that he contracted unwise liabilities; it took but one bad crop to bring about an inextricable predicament. By the beginning of 1882 it became obvious that they would have to go into liquidation. The Létinois family left, it is said, for Belgium. Verlaine stayed on to sell the farm. His mother, at news of the failure, hastened to join him.

This time Verlaine went to Paris. He renewed acquaintance with some of his old friends. Considering the fact that *Paris-Moderne* was already printing some of his verses to Mérat in their July 25, 1882 issue, it seems reasonable to believe that he arrived in Paris no later than July 1.

What was he going to do? He considered a teaching post at the university. But, Delahaye reports, he was too unsure of passing the competitive examination. He determined to initiate steps to regain a position in the Hôtel de Ville. With the help of his friend Lepelletier, he made up a résumé and proceeded to take steps. He had never been dismissed. In 1871, he had simply stopped performing his duties. He might therefore hope for reinstatement. But he had worked for the Commune, and he had the record of his divorce and imprisonment against him. Once set in motion, proceedings lasted from October 1882 until April 1883, and ended in failure. The reason is apparent when one learns that on November 28, 1882, the attorney general attached to the Brussels court sent the Seine Prefecture a letter summarizing the trial of 1873 and referring to the report of the doctors. Society defends itself well and does not forgive.

Verlaine's biographer must attach the greatest importance to this failure. Edmond Lepelletier, who was the poet's best friend at the time, has emphasized this. The government's refusal blocked for Verlaine the path he had been following for seven years. He felt trapped in the net of fate and poverty. It was then, and only then, that he renounced hope of an orderly, middle-class life. He plunged into adventure.

Lucien had come back with his parents to rejoin him. They lived at 14 Rue de Paris in Ivry, and Verlaine at 5 Rue du Parchamp in Boulogne. First, Lucien had found a job at the Institution Esnault, 54 Rue d'Aguesseau in Boulogne; Delahaye had taught there. Then the young man went to work in an industrial establishment. To help Monsieur Esnault, who was something of a friend, out of difficulty, Verlaine took Létinois's place for a while. He ate at the director's table and was not discontented. Even after he had left the institution, he remained in Boulogne for some time. During his free hours Lucien came to see him.

Verlaine ended up settling with his mother in a small apartment at 17 Rue de la Roquette. These initial months of his return to Paris should not be confused with the dreadful years that were to follow. This was not a period of destitution, nor even of poverty. Madame Verlaine had come with the family furniture. The apartment was well lit and cheerful. Moréas described it before Delahaye: simple curtains, provincial middle-class furnishings; on the walls, First Empire pastels, a bleeding, awkward, and sentimental Christ figure by Nouveau. In front of the window, a desk. On shelves a small library where ascetic treatises mingled with libertine works. Madame Verlaine has changed little in temperament or appearance. Only a few more wrinkles, says Delahaye. Her eyes are still lively. She is still animated and engaging. She has made friends very quickly in the neighborhood. And if one cares to picture and understand the Verlaine of 1882, one may linger over the fine photograph he had taken at that time. Truly a record of prime importance. Nothing of the faun's head we will one day see. A dignified, commanding look. An aristocratic baldness. The beard short and neat. The gaze firm and direct. In 1882 Verlaine is at his most attractive and impressive.

An unforeseen occurrence suddenly upset his plans. On April 3, 1883, Lucien Létinois came down with typhoid fever and was taken to the Hôpital de la Pitié. Apprized of this some time later, Verlaine rushed to see him. He found his friend completely delirious and calling his name. On April 7, young Lucien died. Behind the hearse, which was draped in white, Verlaine wept: "As for a young girl! He well deserved it," he said to someone beside him.

He expressed the depth of his grief in moving terms:

> *Cela dura six ans, puis l'ange s'envola.*
> *Dès lors je vais hagard et comme ivre: voilà.*

> It lasted six years, then the angel flew away.
> Since then I go on gaunt, as drunk: no more to say.

But it should be observed that at exactly this date the proceedings for his reinstatement fell through. This dual misfortune explains the sad events to follow.

4 · Last Years

On July 30, 1883, at the office of Maître Sabot, notary of the Batignolles district, Verlaine's mother bought from the Létinois, for the sum of 3,500 francs, the tiny property they owned in Coulommes. It took several weeks to make arrangements for taking possession. Finally, on September 20, Verlaine left Paris, passed briefly through Arras, and went to settle in Coulommes. Once again, he was going to try to remake his life with a small farming enterprise. Lepelletier, who is quite rightly astonished by so irrational an undertaking, is convinced that it was Madame Verlaine's idea, and that she had become disturbed at seeing her son unsuccessful, after six months, in finding a position in Paris. Delahaye is more categorical: it was Madame Verlaine who insisted that Verlaine return to the country, and he obeyed, with the feeling that his mother was making a mistake.

This stay in Coulommes was to last a little more than twenty months, until June 1885. Later, when he recounted the story of his life, Verlaine pinpointed this as the precise moment when he abandoned his many attempts to lead a life of dignity and virtue. The proper life up to that point, he said, but after that, the fast life. There is no doubt, in fact, that that is when he gave way. To drunkenness, first of all. But also to those affairs which, one suspects, cross his life at a number of points, but which he succeeded, for the most part, in concealing. In Coulommes he makes hardly any further effort at dissemblance. He even has, we are told, a number of alarming types come from Paris. Circulating about him are a number of "young rascals with lesbian eyes" and "La Dernière Fête galante" (The Last of Love's Revels) announces, in a gesture of defiance:

L'embarquement pour Sodome et Gomorrhe.

Embarkation for Sodom and Gomorrah.

Later he will tell Cazals that in one week of madness he spent seven thousand francs. In the squalid milieu into which he had plunged, he had a number of adventures. Two scoundrels beat him up one day and robbed him.

Debts piled up. Foreseeing complications, Madame Verlaine, by writ transacted on April 17, 1884, in the office of Maître Chartier, notary in Attigny, gave her son the Coulommes property as a gift, but with a clause of immunity to seizure. At the end of the year, Verlaine found himself with three or four lawsuits on his hands. There was nothing left to do but liquidate the disastrous enterprise. At his Attigny notary's office, on March 8, 1885, he sold his property for the sum of 2,200 francs.

When he came to Paris, he lodged with Courtois, a wine and tobacco seller on Rue de la Roquette, his old neighborhood. On February 9, 1885, he took up residence at Austin's Hotel, Rue d'Amsterdam, near the Gare Saint-Lazare, and there seems to be some foundation to Lepelletier's suspicion that at this time he contemplated fleeing to England. He went back to Coulommes, however. It was there that in a drunken fit he attacked his mother and threatened to kill her. The neighbors brought complaint. On March 24, 1885, he appeared before the court of summary jurisdiction of Vouziers. He was sentenced to a month in jail. When he came out of the house of detention on May 13, 1885, his mother had gone away. He found himself alone, and, for the first time in his life, without resources.

Biographers for a long time remained ignorant of the months that followed his release from jail. It has been supposed that he wandered about on the roads from May until the following October. A notation that De Bouillane de Lacoste has called attention to on the original manuscript of Bonheur (Happiness) proves that on June 13 Verlaine was already in Paris at 6 Cour

Saint-François. Moreover, the poet's *Souvenirs* describe his experiences in the vicinity of Juniville on June 1. Between the time of his release from jail and June 1, it is likely that he went to seek refuge and aid from his old friend, Father Dewez, in the Belgian Ardennes.

His return to Paris in June 1885, was quite different from that of 1882. This time he was destitute. The furniture had been sold in Coulommes. As for capital, only a handful of bonds, about twenty thousand francs worth, which Madame Verlaine was keeping as a last resource, were left. She had forgiven once again and had come to rejoin her son. She had taken a room on the second floor, his room being on the ground floor, right under her.

This boardinghouse, the Hôtel du Midi, in the Cour Saint-François, was a miserable hovel. Living conditions were atrocious. In his room on the ground floor, which had no floorboards or tiling, with light coming only from a kind of chill and seeping shaftway, poor Verlaine was bedridden with hydrarthrosis of the left knee, which had broken out in September. His leg was swollen, the knee stiff, the foot numb. A doctor by the name of Jullien tended the sick man: he had the leg put in a splint. Madame Verlaine devoted herself to taking care of him, unmindful of her own health. She caught cold. On January 21, 1886, she died. The stairway was too narrow for the coffin. It was lowered from the window without her rash and blameworthy son's being able to see for the last time the mother he had loved too much and whom he had dragged with him in his downfall.

Then the Mautés reappeared. On January 25 they had Madame Verlaine's room put under lock and key. They based their claim on the fact that Verlaine had not paid the allowance of twelve hundred francs to which the court had bound him for the upkeep of little Georges. When the sheriff arrived, Verlaine handed over to him the bundle of twenty thousand francs worth of bonds that his mother had left, and which had been concealed under a mattress. A gesture at once noble and insane. For when he had paid Madame Verlaine's burial expenses and settled his bills, the poor man was left with exactly eight hundred francs.

LAST YEARS

He was to live yet another ten years. Biographers have often painted this last period in a single even tone, as if it were but one long and monotonous succession of degradations and miseries. If we are to understand Verlaine, it is important, on the contrary, to distinguish carefully among the particular moments, successive circumstances, and lapses and reforms that make up these ten years.

After the Mautés' heinous action, he found himself bedridden, without resources. His only hope was to recover the fifteen hundred francs owed him for some years by a former curate in Saint-Gervais, and another thousand francs which the notary in Juniville still owed him. The first matter is an obscure one. Lepelletier has said that among the causes of his ruin, Verlaine included the inveigling of an opportunistic and unscrupulous priest. He said, too, that there had been fraud, and that it had deprived Verlaine of his last resources. The person in question was a certain Father Salard. His debt dated at least from the Coulommes period. In September 1884, Verlaine wrote in vain to the archdiocese of Paris. The debt at the time amounted to fifteen hundred francs. In 1888, this recalcitrant debtor still had not paid Verlaine what he owed him. The notary in Juniville showed equally little haste in meeting his obligation to the poet.

At the beginning of July 1886 sores broke out on his legs. Verlaine went to the Tenon Hospital and stayed there until September 2. One can only believe that hope and energy were deep-rooted in him. A little cash on hand, and expectation of the sums owed him by the priest and the notary, sufficed to give him courage. He returned to the same wretched quarters in the Hôtel du Midi. But he had to go to the hospital again on November 3. This time it was the Broussais Hospital that took him in. His left knee was completely immobilized; the sores would not heal. Dr. Nélaton, who was in attendance, said that nothing could be done. He attributed the sores to an old syphilitic infection. A letter of this period reveals the violence of the sick man's despair.

He had sworn, on leaving the Cour Saint-François, never to return. When he came out of the Broussais Hospital in Febru-

ary 1887, however, he had to return to that miserable shelter.
The year of 1887 was one of the greatest possible distress, and
Verlaine was not to know for the rest of his life such profound
and total destitution. "Misery and almost the hangman," he
wrote of the horrible period of March–April 1887. He contemplated suicide. The hospital prevented him from it. His publisher and friend, Léon Vanier, had consulted with Dr. Nélaton.
On April 19, he entered the Cochin Hospital, and in May he
was transferred to the Vincennes Hospital. His fears of dying
were dispelled. But the future was still frightening. He thought
only of the salvation that he had at all costs to achieve.

From hospital to hospital, from Vincennes to Tenon and from
Tenon back to Vincennes, he lived through the first days of
September. They were, according to his description, "the plunge,
the thrashing in the underbrush, the near-annihilation, half-
sinking, half-drowning." The correspondence, once one has
established the exact date and order of the letters, confirms the
poet's recollections. Around the fifteenth of September 1887,
Verlaine quite literally nearly died of hunger. Some friends
came to his rescue, and Coppée sent fifty francs. This act of
charity, which came just in time, enabled Verlaine to survive
another few days, and around the twenty-fifth of September
the Broussais Hospital took him in once again. He stayed
there for the entire winter.

It was in 1888 that people in the Latin Quarter began to see
a man limping about, rapping the sidewalk with his cane.
Every day he walked up and down the Boulevard Saint-Michel,
escorted by a phalanx of young poets, spending hours in the
cafés, the Soleil d'Or, the Cluny, the François I. The pictures
we have of him show that it was during that year that his face
assumed its final appearance—that face which had something
both of Socrates and of a faun, in which could be discerned
consciousness of genius, scorn for the proprieties, keenness of
intellect, and formidable sensuality.

He divided his time between hospitals and furnished rooms
in the Latin Quarter. He had become a regular patient at
Broussais. After Dr. Jullien and Dr. Nélaton, Dr. Chauffard had
befriended him. He sometimes took the poet out for a meal in
some modest restaurant. The Lasègue ward, to which he had

been assigned, became for a time a kind of salon where he received admirers. The administration assigned to the same ward all of the half-starved and ailing poets who turned up. Cazals claims that it got to the point where four of the ten beds in the ward were occupied by foster children of the Muses.

Verlaine worked while in the hospital. During long bouts of insomnia he composed the poems for *Bonheur* and for *Liturgies intimes* (Inner Devotions). He had obtained the privilege of having a bedlamp. But at other times he spent entire days in extreme pain and at such times could neither get out of bed, read, nor work. The condition of his leg did not improve. In 1887, he spoke of his "terrible lameness," and complained of the blisters and chafing that it caused. His heart showed signs of weakening, and the doctors had discovered a pericardial condition. By the end of 1888 he could hardly walk.

When he was not in the hospital, he lodged in one or another of the hotels on the Left Bank. He had left the Cour Saint-François with no intention of returning. According to Cazals, he first went to find lodgings in Rue de la Huchette. Then he moved to the Hôtel Royer-Collard, at number 14 of the street of that name. A rooming agency card shows that he was there on March 25, 1888. He stayed there until the end of November. He had become conscious of his growing fame and received his most ardent admirers in his room every Wednesday. These soirées, simple but comfortable, sometimes brought out as many as forty guests. Villiers, Barrès, Vicaire, Ary Renan, Rachilde, and Moréas were to be seen there, not to mention Cazals, Jules Tellier, Paterne Berrichon, the novelist D'Argis, and Fernand Clerget.

Verlaine moved from the Hôtel Royer-Collard around the end of November 1888, to the Hôtel des Nations at 216 Rue Saint-Jacques. He has described in a few graphic lines the dreadful stairwell, the flight of steps with its supports of bare tree stumps painted blood red, and the candle kept burning on a window sill to light the way for the poet's guests. For these "Wednesdays" continued, accompanied sometimes by beer and sometimes by sugared water and rum. Very severe rheumatic pains forced Verlaine, in December 1888, to go back to Broussais. When he came out in February 1889, Maurice Barrès found him a room at the Hôtel de Lisbonne, 4 Rue de Vaugirard. This was a comfortable hotel where Gambetta had once stayed. Verlaine's great friend at this period, the young painter Cazals, and his wife, occupied a room with bed-alcove and kitchen there. The poet made do with just a room. But he often shared the family meal, and Marie Cazals tended his leg with friendly devotion. In the hotel dining room he made the acquaintance of a number of congenial regulars, among whom numbered several young and lively ladies. The hotel manager was fond of poetry and looked with indulgence on the comings and goings of the poet's overly numerous friends; the "Wednesdays" were still being held. However, when she attempted to put an end to other kinds of visits that might reflect on the hotel's good name, Verlaine left.

In February 1890, after a six-month stay at Broussais, we find him in the Hôtel des Mines, 125 Boulevard Saint-Michel. This was a sober-looking and perfectly comfortable establishment. It had a middle-class clientele, and the atmosphere of the neighborhood as well as that of the hotel reminded one more of the Saint-Sulpice area than the Latin Quarter. This remote location was discouraging to the "Wednesday" regulars. They dropped out of sight. Verlaine did not complain. This was one of the periods in his life when he worked hardest, and he was able to complete a number of old pieces that had been drafted some time earlier. He entertained himself by going to meetings of *La Plume* at the further end of the Boulevard Saint-Michel.

Whoever examines the details of his life closely finds it rather less disordered than legend has it. It is clear that little by little Verlaine was on the upgrade. He had hit bottom in 1887. The following year had still been terrible. That was when Léon Bloy found the author of *Sagesse* prey to dreadful despair and contemplating suicide. At that time Verlaine, encouraged by Bloy and by Huysmans, had hoped that his old friend Father Dewez would take him in at his house in Corbion, in the Belgian Ardennes. But Father Dewez replied that he was not a person to be easily duped, and there was nothing for Léon Bloy to do but send him an eloquent and abusive letter.

At the Hôtel de Lisbonne and the Hôtel des Mines, however,

Verlaine, whose resources were slowly increasing, was able to make life a bit less uncertain for himself. He rose early, often at three o'clock in the morning, and lit his lamp. He wrote. Sometimes the poem was finished by eight o'clock, and the poet would take it to Vanier, his publisher. He would continue to work until the fatal apéritif hour. At that hour he would leave his room and go to one of his usual cafés. There he would meet some of his friends to whom he would generously offer drinks. Expense statements, drawn up by his landlords, have been found. Meals do not amount to much. But "rounds of drinks" show up every day—in one establishment alone, an average of twenty to twenty-five francs worth a day—and to really appreciate this figure, it should be remembered that an ordinary worker earned five francs a day at the time. In examining these accounts, one has the impression that Verlaine drank far too many apéritifs but that he ruined himself, above all, by buying drinks for his friends.

Why should we imagine him as perpetually drunk? Albert Lantoine, who saw him several times around this time—at the *Chat Noir*—describes him as lucid and reserved, hands leaning on his cane, attracting little attention: the only thing that struck him, writes this observer, was his limpid and marvelously child-like gaze. The numerous sketches that Cazals has left us—in which we see Verlaine in cafés—confirm Lantoine's impression; and Ernest Raynaud has said that these drawings are, for appraising Verlaine properly, the surest and most accurate of documents.

In collating the various reports, one meets with great perplexity. Some people, who did not approach him but only crossed his path in the Latin Quarter, retain a terrible recollection of him. André Gide saw him, drunk and in a rage, surrounded by jeering urchins, holding up his suspenderless trousers with both hands. Valéry has retained impressions of the same kind. Jules Renard saw him at a *Plume* dinner on March 8, 1892. "The appalling Verlaine," he wrote, "a mournful Socrates and a befouled Diogenes—dog- and hyena-like."

But those who penetrated his life intimately have spoken of him in another way altogether. They have described what he retained of pride, of refinement, of courage during the very years in which he seemed to have let himself go. Moréas has said that his true side was his cavalier, Spanish-cape side. A Swiss writer who saw a great deal of him at the time praised his humor. It was, he said, at the basis of his nature—rich, profuse, fertile, spontaneous. Rachilde writes for his part: "He has been too often pictured with his elbows on a café table in front of a glass of absinthe: he was born a man of inner feeling and discerning taste." In contrast to those biographers who over-draw and insist on seeing nothing but degradation, let us recall these most perceptive words of Cazals: "This old, ingenuous terror of a child . . ." and those of Maurice Baud which echo them: "He was an *enfant terrible* whom all things distressed, and captivated, or delighted."

The curious thing is that his dreadful experiences had moulded and reshaped his face, had conferred on him a kind of beauty. Rachilde noted his terrible gaze—intense, brooding, a sovereign's gaze. His face was marvelously mobile and expressive. It would change in an instant from mischievous gaiety to Jupiterian rage. This man of worn-out body and threadbare costume had, in his fallen state, the dignity of a prince or a struck-down Titan. André Gide said that when drunk, Verlaine was "tremendous."

It is not an indiscreet inquiry to wish to ascertain the place that pleasure occupied in Verlaine's life. In the Cour Saint-François, he lived with a number of women. One of them, a certain Marie Gambier, was his companion for several months: she is the Princess Roukine of *Parallèlement* (Parallelly). One may guess at other feminine presences, the first since Mathilde. But one need not conclude from this that Verlaine denies himself forbidden sensual pleasure. The obscene collection *Hombres* (Men) was written in 1891, and it would be hard to believe it was written in jest. One curious Latin Quarter type, André Salis—nicknamed "Bibi la Purée"—confided to André Billy that he had at one time had corydonesque relations with Verlaine.

It is nonetheless true that a number of women turn up in Verlaine's life at this period. A certain Caroline Teisen, a German or Lorraine woman of thirty, vacuous and easygoing, is referred to. The names of Andrée, Marie, and that of Lily (who may be the same person as Caroline Teisen) are mentioned. At

the very time the poet was just about settled, he managed to
sleep on twenty successive days with twenty different women
picked up at random. A police record dated February 9, 1892,
indicates that he "maintains his usual intercourse with prosti-
tutes."

At this period, however, he was already sharing his time in
fairly regular fashion between two women, Philomène Boudin
and Eugénie Krantz. He had known the former since 1887. She
was a peasant girl who, after being seduced and then jilted, had
sought refuge in Paris. According to Lepelletier, she was ami-
able, sweet-tempered, and sisterly, with the manners of the
poorer middle class. She was still beautiful and retained, despite
her forty years, a certain youthfulness. Her single fault was
that of having a lover, some say, alas, a pimp, who held the
poet in some kind of respect, who even affected to take him
under his wing, but who had no qualms about robbing him in
collusion with the sweet and gentle Philomène.

In February 1891, Verlaine had taken up lodgings in the
Hôtel de Montpellier, 18 Rue Descartes. The manager's name
was Paul Lacan and, despite this name, it seems one should
identify him with that broad-shouldered and brute-faced Ameri-
can of whom Cazals has spoken. Philomène was in league with
Lacan. It is clear from several accounts that during the spring
of 1891 she was the poet's habitual companion.

But in May he met another woman, Eugénie Krantz. During
the last years of the Empire she had been a figure in the Paris
smart set. She had even been, subsequently, the mistress of Con-
stans. But she had aged and had become as ugly "as the seven
deadly sins," and by the same token had settled down. No one
knew of her having a lover. She was a good housekeeper and
earned enough to live on by working at the sewing machine
in the Belle Jardinière department store. This guise of thrifty
lower middle-class lady captivated Verlaine despite the woman's
rapaciousness and her quarrelsome and jealous temper.

According to one well-informed biography based on still unpublished documents, Verlaine, beginning in May 1891, surrendered to this new love with reckless passion. He ignored
all his doctors' prescriptions and soon found himself penniless
and crippled in every limb. Then began those grotesquely the-

atrical scenes that were to remove what small dignity his life retained. Philomène, dismissed, kept a watch on her rival and went to the point of confronting her in the street. She had her spies and Eugénie had hers. Bibi la Purée carried Eugénie's messages; Paul Lacan was Philomène's "supporter."

For love of Eugénie Krantz, Verlaine spent all his money. He could no longer pay the rent on his room. On September 21, 1891, Lacan refused him entrance to the hotel. Verlaine was drunk. He had a friend, Henri Chollin, with him. The three men fought, and Verlaine went off to lodge at number 15 on the same street, in a hotel frequented by pimps and their charges. After this he wrote: "Mademoiselle Krantz, who is worthy of every confidence and whom I like very much . . . ."

From then on he divided his time between the two women. Eugénie's reign lasted, with the exception of a few periods of unfaithfulness, until the middle of 1892. It is probable that at that time she abandoned him. He was destitute once again. He went back to Broussais, and Philomène turned up again. At this point he inveighed against "Mademoiselle Eumenides," as he called her. It was Philomène who came to Broussais, during the winter of 1892–1893, to visit the ailing Verlaine. Her rival, however, had not renounced her intention of winning him back. When he left the hospital in February 1893, he went to live at 9 Rue des Fossés Saint-Jacques—that is, with Eugénie. The latter had once again become his "decidedly best friend."

Verlaine's health did not improve. In November 1891, he was again forced to go back to Broussais. He was suffering from rheumatism, heart murmurs, the onset of diabetes, and the final stages of syphilis. He went back to the hospital the following August and again in December 1892. In May 1893, the infectious erysipelas of his left leg worsened. He was in great pain. He resigned himself in June to asking for readmission to Broussais. His friend, Dr. Chauffard, judged the patient's condition to be more serious than he himself thought it was. In a short time, indeed, Verlaine became delirious. It was feared that the outcome would be fatal. The crisis passed, but Verlaine's leg was covered with infectious abcesses which had to be lanced. His heart ailment prevented him from sleeping.

During all this time Eugénie showed up hardly at all. Philomène, on the other hand, was attentive, a constant and affectionate visitor. Verlaine conceived the plan of marrying her. He now referred to her as "my wife, Philomène." The marriage was to take place upon his return from England where he had gone to give some lectures. But Eugénie was keeping a sharp eye out. She was able to enlighten Verlaine on certain of her rival's less creditable actions, and it was once again at her house —at 187 Rue Saint-Jacques—that he went to live in December 1893. It was a sorry room on the sixth floor. The floor was of red tiles. Scarcely any light penetrated this gloomy retreat. The furniture consisted of two armchairs, four straight chairs, and a solid mahogany bed. A sewing machine attested the presence and activity of Eugénie.

After the squalid room at the Hôtel de Montpellier, this wretched accommodation on Rue Saint-Jacques is positive proof of the downward turn matters had taken. The poet, who from 1886 to 1890 had been on the upgrade, fell back once more —through the agency of Philomène, who robbed him, and Eugénie, who exploited him. It was not as if he were not earning any money. His books were selling well; poetry lovers fought for his autograph. He was asked to lecture in Holland (November 1892), in Belgium (March 1893), and in Lorraine and England (November 1893). These tours brought him sums that would set a good number of present-day lecturers dreaming. His English tour brought him fifteen hundred francs.* On returning from Belgium, he had a thousand francs in his wallet.

If the situation was not even further improved, it was because he spent money wildly. In 1890, Léon Deschamp, who did so much to help Verlaine when he was in difficult straits, wrote René Ghil that the poet had just spent six hundred francs in the space of a few days. "He is on a terrible spree," he explained. In England he disappeared for two days and came back without a penny. The thousand francs he earned in Belgium were stolen from him upon his return to Paris. In a letter to Philomène he reproaches her for having "spent or set aside three thousand francs without profit to himself."

In April 1894 the condition of his leg had become so grave

* More than 3,000 New Francs. [Tr.]

that Dr. Jullien put him in the Saint-Louis Hospital, in the Gabriel Pavilion, as a paying patient. There, for a time, he led a fairly pleasant life and began to work again. Eugénie had abandoned him. She was now living at 48 Rue du Cardinal-Lemoine. On coming out of the hospital, he wrote her with a view to taking up life together again. He vowed he could not do without her despite her terrible disposition. She did not yield. He had received some money while in the hospital. Because Eugénie didn't want him any more, he went to live in the Hôtel de Lisbonne where he had once known better days. He rented a room with a fine view of the Luxembourg garden. Eugénie made scenes. She tore up some of the poet's papers and refused to return to him certain objects she had kept at her place.

He entered the hospital for the last time in December 1894. He came out on the arm of Philomène whom he jokingly called "his beloved widow." Abandoned by her in a hotel room after a dreadful quarrel, he wandered for several days from furnished room to furnished room. He wrote at the time: "No more woman, nor women." But Eugénie took him up again. We find him in February, in the garret she occupied at 16 Rue Saint-Victor, bedridden by a relapse: an abcess had broken out on his left foot. She tended him devotedly and his health seemed to improve. Order returned to his finances. More and more money was coming in. At the end of September, the household settled at 39 Rue Descartes, in an apartment with two rooms and a kitchen. The dining room overlooked the back, but the other room was well lit by two windows facing the street. Eugénie bought a few pieces of furniture, a sofa, and some drapes. She also bought a can of gold paint, and Verlaine conscientiously set about covering his chairs and even his tobacco jar with it. He took a childish joy in this return to modest comfort and showed visitors the mustache comb that Eugénie had given him. She even had a cleaning woman, Zélie, come in. The poet now wore clean linen and slept between white sheets.

It seemed, says Cazals, that he had finally attained peace and quiet. He had pretty much given up drinking, and absinthe no longer tempted him. There was, perhaps, a bit of infantilism in all this, a touch of premature senility. That was Lepelletier's

impression, and Charles Donos speaks of Verlaine's failing
faculties. Certain anecdotes, however, lead one to believe that
his mind still remained as alert and nimble as ever in a body
in which the passions had been stilled. Eugénie watched over
him, his "ill-natured old keeper, with her Tillie the Toiler airs."
She kept a jealous eye out for the poet. But there was no longer
any question of his thinking of wandering.

At the beginning of December 1895, his leg began to swell up
again. He went out, however, on December 7, to have dinner in
an expensive restaurant—Foyot's—to which Robert de Montesquiou had had the rather grotesque idea of inviting him. One
must point out, moreover, that the worthy count paid for the
dinner but did not bother to attend. His secretary, Yturri, sat in
for him. On Christmas Day, stomach pains and a neglected
cold obliged Verlaine to keep to his room. Dr. Parisot prescribed a strict diet. On Sunday, January 5, 1896, Verlaine had
a touch of delirium. His fever did not go down until that afternoon. On Tuesday the seventh, he felt better. He got up. He
ate dinner with Le Rouge and his wife. The meal was genial
and cheerful. Delahaye, however, who had come, became concerned. He came close to bringing up the subject of the sacraments. But Verlaine set the conversation on another tack.
That evening the fever returned. Eugénie panicked. Then what
happened? Was there a last quarrel wherein the poor man,
while struggling, was thrown to the floor? More likely, Verlaine,
obliged to get out of bed, could not keep on his feet and fell.
Eugénie was not strong enough to lift him. Some have said
that she abandoned him, nude, on the icy tiling of the floor.
Actually, she wrapped him up in blankets, put an eiderdown
quilt over him, then went off to a neighbor's house to weep.

Before daybreak, the sick man was lifted back into bed. But
he was done for. Bronchial pneumonia had set in. Dr. Parisot
was called. He came in haste and judged Verlaine's condition
desperate. Cazals and the Le Rouges assisted the distraught
Eugénie. Dr. Chauffard came too. He prescribed mustard
plasters. Shortly thereafter, Verlaine went into a coma. All day
January 8, 1896, numerous friends dropped by to inquire at the
sorry lodging on Rue Descartes. At eight o'clock, when they
came by again, Verlaine had just died.

The obsequies were impressive. Barrès, Coppée, Lepelletier, Mendès, and Montesquiou were the pallbearers. Charles Widor was at the organ. The ministry of Beaux-Arts was represented. Several thousand people followed the hearse from Saint-Etienne-du-Mont to the Batignolles cemetery. Speeches were made over the grave by Coppée, Barrès, Kahn, Mallarmé, Mendès, and Moréas.

Part Two · Works

5 · *The First Collections*

The earliest verses we have of Verlaine date from 1858. He was then a ninth-grade student. We have others, more numerous, that he wrote in his last year at the lycée. Let us set aside his few translations of Latin poets into French verse; these are merely exercises. In the other pieces, in which the youthful poet was attempting original composition, one discerns the early influences he underwent and certain tendencies that were already taking shape. His masters are obviously Victor Hugo, from 1858 on, and Baudelaire, from 1861 on. The first name is not surprising. That of Baudelaire is somewhat more surprising, for at that date his *Fleurs du Mal* was a very recent publication, the exacerbated expression of feelings that were still foreign to most contemporaries, a book that a schoolboy might manage to read only on the sly.

What the Lycée Bonaparte schoolboy undoubtedly detected in Baudelaire, what he first appreciated, was the troubled sensuality that exists in even those who strive after a visionary purity. "Aspiration," written in 1861, expresses in a still naïve manner this dream of flight beyond life and its ugliness toward an ideal of beauty and love. A flight

> *Loin de tout ce qui vit, loin des hommes, encor*
> *Plus loin des femmes.*

> Far from all that lives, far from men, farther
> Still from women.

One is tempted to smile at these verses by a seventeen-year-old boy, except that one sees inscribed in them the outlines of his fate.

Right after graduation from the lycée, in 1863, Verlaine came in contact with the world of men of letters. Louis-Xavier de Ricard had just founded, in March, his *Revue du progrès moral*. One of Verlaine's friends, Miot-Frochot, took him to the offices of the *Revue*. Ricard agreed to publish, in the August 1863 issue, a satirical sonnet, "Monsieur Prudhomme." Verlaine and his friend Lepelletier from then on were very much involved with Ricard.

One must be careful not to make the mistake of supposing, in consequence, that this small group of friends professed the principles that were, three years later, to become those of the Parnassians. The *Revue du progrès moral* was very far from supporting the theses of the Art for Art's Sake school. It abused Gautier, Flaubert, even Vigny. It extolled moral and scientific poetry, that devoted to progress. In that same year of 1863, Ricard's *Chants de l'aube* (Songs of Dawn) was printed. In it he names his masters. They are Quinet, Népomucène, Lemercier, and Dupontavice de Heussey. To an admirer of Baudelaire these views must have seemed strange. But Verlaine was doubtless willing to overlook certain peculiarities. He let himself be swept along by Ricard; he became a Republican and thought that the time would come when action and vision would be reconciled, when poets would be the guides of humanity, when life would coincide with beauty. In March 1864, the *Revue du progrès moral* was suppressed "on the grounds of outrage against religious morals" and for having spoken on matters of political economy without authorization. L.-X. de Ricard was sentenced to eight months in jail. Verlaine and Lepelletier remained loyal to him. They were again there to support him after he had paid his penalty.

It was at this time, during the last weeks of 1864, that they made the acquaintance of Catulle Mendès; the latter chanced to be living on the same floor as Ricard. Since 1861 Mendès had been playing the role of animator to a number of young people. He gathered about him Glatigny, Sully-Prudhomme, Villiers, Dierx, and Hérédia. He represented a school of thought quite different from Ricard's. Thanks to him, the tradition of the fanciful was carried on. Gautier and Banville were his gods. In 1863, in *Philoméla*, he had imitated Heine, had written pagan verses, and professed a doctrine of art in which it is not difficult to detect the marked influence of Gautier, much stronger than that of Baudelaire. L.-X. de Ricard was soon won over, and he who had up to that point denounced the mandarins of Art for Art's Sake, in December 1864 wrote a poem to the Venus de Milo, to that serene beauty, untroubled by passions. In it one might read the following lines, in which a word occurs that was soon to become very popular:

> *Poëte, garde ainsi ton âme intacte et fière;*
> *Que ton esprit, vêtu d'impassibilité,*
> *Marche à travers la vie au but qui l'a tenté.*

> Poet, so keep your soul intact and proud,
> That your spirit may, wrapped in impassibility,
> Proceed through life to the goal that drew it on.

Verlaine committed himself to the same path. He too became an *impassible*.

His circle of acquaintances grew. In 1865 he made the acquaintance of Sully-Prudhomme, whom he met at the studio of a painter named Brown, who was then linked with Massol and the Morale Indépendante group. He made friends with Anatole France at the home of a man named Destailleurs, whom he had known at the Lycée Condorcet; soon after, he met France again at Ricard's. At the same time, certain books he was reading were changing his orientation. One day he had found, in a bookstore on Rue Voltaire, Glatigny's *Vignes folles* (Wild Vines). Then he had read *Philoméla* by his new friend Mendès. These two collections, he himself said, were for a long time his bedside reading. They acquainted him with a form of poetry that was much less concerned with social progress, much more fanciful and free than Ricard's. When he met Glatigny in the Café de Suède, he struck up a friendship with that good fellow whose talent he held in high esteem.

Ricard had just founded a new magazine, *L'Art*. The title alone, by comparison with that of the *Revue du progrès moral*, clearly indicates the road traveled and the direction taken.

Mendès may have picked it out. Ricard, however, was prime mover of the enterprise. Verlaine worked closely with him. He contributed two poems and two noteworthy critical studies on Baudelaire and Barbey d'Aurevilly to the magazine. Ricard was still his guide and mentor. Together with Lepelletier and France, they comprised a group. There was no question, at that date, of their joining forces under the leadership of Leconte de Lisle. In a letter dated March 1865, Hérédia lists the faithful who meet at the master's house. He does not mention either Ricard, or Verlaine, or France, or Lepelletier.

L'Art was going badly. In December 1865 a new editor was needed. One now sees how closely linked Verlaine was to Ricard. He had a friend by the name of Boutier, a poet and amateur violinist. The latter knew a bookseller in Passage Choiseul—Alphonse Lemerre. Boutier put Verlaine in touch with him, and Verlaine in turn brought in Ricard and Lepelletier. The deal was settled. It was settled, one should note, without any consultation with either Leconte de Lisle or Mendès. It was only when *L'Art* in turn failed and was, on Mendès initiative, replaced by *Parnasse contemporain* that Ricard's influence was overthrown and the real Parnassian school came into being. Verlaine contributed to the first issue (March–June 1866) of *Parnasse*. He published eight pieces of verse in it. But he was already preparing his first collection for publication.

If we attempt to understand Verlaine at this moment in his life, we may observe a number of tendencies that are already pronounced. The young man is a Baudelairian, in spite of Ricard, Mendès, Leconte de Lisle, and even, perhaps, of Baudelaire himself. He has a distinct taste for macabre humor. In "Fadaises" (Foolishness) he has fun with a kind of doleful madrigal whose meaning does not become apparent until the last line: his Lady is death. "L'Enterrement" (Burial) is characteristic:

> *Je ne sais rien de gai comme un enterrement . . .*
>
> I know of nothing as gay as a burial . . .

and Lepelletier tells us that he had to stop Verlaine from including this piece in *Poèmes saturniens* (Saturnine Poems).

At the same time the doctrine of Art for Art's Sake to which he rallied in 1865, takes blunt and dogmatic form with him. His "Vers dorés" (Gilded Lines), which appeared in *Parnasse* in 1866, clearly expresses this rigidity:

> *L'Art ne veut point de pleurs et ne transige pas . . .*

> Art wants no tears and does not compromise . . .

One descries the doctrinarian in him. He is such in his art and in his philosophy. He vents equal scorn on the sentimental out-pourings of a certain kind of romanticism and the vague religiosity then in style in the democratic camp. "Les Dieux" (The Gods) and "Sur le Calvaire" (On Calvary) express an attitude of militant revolt against all religions. One would be tempted to see in this dogmatism a proof of forcefulness and stability if the Baudelairian backdrops and the macabre sense of humor did not enable one to discern the confusion, the gloomy pre-occupations, and the anguish underneath.

POÈMES SATURNIENS

At the beginning of 1866, Verlaine was putting together a volume of verse. First he thought of calling it *Poèmes et sonnets*. He anticipated publication at a later date of a second collection to be called *Les Danaïdes. Epigrammes, études antiques* (The Danaides. Epigrams, Classical Studies). Then he changed the title he had planned to give the first book to *Poèmes saturniens*.

Today we have come to see that these poems are not the work of a devoted disciple of Leconte de Lisle and that Parnassian orthodoxy plays a smaller role in them than was at first believed. Parnassian to be sure, and directly inspired by Leconte de Lisle are the "Orpheus" and "Alkaios" (Alcaeus) poems in it. One readily believes as well that the few words of Hindu in the Prologue were inspired by Leconte de Lisle's *Poèmes antiques*. On this point, however, the influences already show themselves to be complex. J. H. Bornecque has discovered that the most Hindu, and the only Hindu poem in the *Poèmes saturniens*— "Çavitrî"—comes directly from a Romantic collection, *La Pléiade*. In L.-X. de Ricard's *Chants de l'aube* one finds a good many Hindu words. Ricard was the nephew of an Orientalist, Pauthier, and was interested in the poetry of India. In October

1864, he wrote a poem called "Açoka." If Verlaine speaks of the "Ganga," Ricard, too, had used a feminine turn of phrase in speaking of the sacred river: he had, in his *Ciel, Rue et Foyer* (Sky, Street and Home), called it "the white goddess." The word *padma*, which Verlaine employs, is found in the same collection: "Brow wreathed with padmas. . . ." The poet's correspondence shows that he had read the *Ramayana* in 1865. Who dares say that Ricard's recommendations in this choice of reading carried less weight than the example set by Leconte de Lisle?

The same complexity occurs on a point of cardinal importance for the accurate interpretation of the *Poèmes saturniens*. These poems state uncompromisingly, and with passionate conviction, the doctrine of Pure Art and Impassibility. The name that first comes to mind is that of Leconte de Lisle. This is almost certainly a mistake. For Verlaine had expounded this doctrine the year before in his *L'Art* articles, and in reference to Baudelaire. With great boldness he had affirmed the secondary nature of Baudelairian satanism and had laid the emphasis on his doctrine of art: the mutual independence of the beautiful, the true, and the useful; distrust in place of passion; scorn for inspiration, that prop, and of the inspired, those charlatans. In *Fleurs du Mal* Verlaine admired not so much the touching confidences imparted, but the mastery, the icy calm from which the poet never departed, even when his emotion was at its height—the phlegmatic insolence of the *poète dandy*, the knowing and deliberate character of a work in which not one word, phrase, or rhyme was accidental, where everything, down to the tiniest detail, was the result of long meditation.

That is the real doctrine that inspires him, and Baudelaire is his master. He would doubtless be astonished if one were to tell him he was Leconte de Lisle's disciple. He probably admires the latter. He has read the Preface to the *Poèmes barbares* (Barbarous Poems) of 1862, which takes the poetry of confession and elegiacal Romanticism so much to task. He extols the beauty of Leconte de Lisle's verses. But the qualities he finds in them are still Baudelairian: these rocklike verses, he says, "reverberate like distant thunderings that never clap, by virtue of that supreme artistic law that any outburst is a discord, and that beauty lies in harmony."

When one isolates the unconscious imitations and echoes which the pieces in *Poèmes saturniens* betray, the various influences to which Verlaine is subject come to light. First and foremost among these, of course, is Victor Hugo—but in a diffuse fashion such as one would doubtless find in the work of any young poet of that generation. As for Leconte de Lisle, several unmistakable echoes suffice to prove that Verlaine had his work very much in mind at the time. But the influence of Banville and, especially, of Gautier, is much stronger. Verlaine gives the impression of being saturated in *Mademoiselle de Maupin,* of having a thorough and detailed knowledge of its themes, images, and turns of phrase. He often brings to mind as well Aloysius Bertrand and his volume of prose poems, *Gaspard de la nuit* (Sneak in the Night). Finally, among the young poets, there are two in whom Verlaine has discovered kindred spirits and whose lines run through his head: Ricard and Glatigny. A close reading of the *Poèmes saturniens* reveals constant and distinct echoes of both poets. They add to the all-pervasive influence of Baudelaire a more youthful and ingenuous note.

The book was entitled *Poèmes saturniens,* and this title echoed a line from Baudelaire and also, perhaps, a sentence from *Mademoiselle de Maupin.* The *poèmes* were admissions of anxiety and despair, the plaint of a soul incapable of controlling its fate, of escaping from the exigencies of a blood pervasive as poison and hot as running lava. An extremely demanding but quickly spent sensual passion. Vague but hopeless desires. A longing for purity and peace amidst the dismal pleasures of the flesh. It is a great temptation to think that these plaints are, on the poet's part, a confession of his anguish on the brink of great catastrophes.

If one is to agree with J. H. Bornecque's critical edition of the *Poèmes saturniens,* a book singularly rich in learning and of most subtle intelligence, one should go even further—and admit that in this volume Verlaine allowed the unfortunate passion he felt for his cousin, Elisa Moncomble, later Madame Dujardin, to show through. Many of the pieces in the collection would, according to this interpretation, refer to the young woman. It would be she, the beloved of refreshing voice, who asks the poet what his happiest day was; she, the woman of pure and virtuous soul whom he begs to come to his aid and save him. The little garden the poet visits "after three years" would be the garden in Lécluse, seen in 1862 and again in 1865.

This alluring interpretation does not hesitate to contradict reputable accounts. Edmond Lepelletier, who was at this period Verlaine's closest friend, who saw him daily, who according to his own report witnessed the birth of most of the poems in the collection, is positive on this point: Verlaine put nothing into the *Poèmes saturniens* except a "concern for dogmatizing, for creating poetics." The whole collection is impersonal. Not one poem can be traced to an actual occurrence, or experienced sensation, or any actual joy or grief. The women to whom some of the verses are addressed have no actual existence. The sadness permeating the collection is a mental fiction—for Verlaine was at this time in good health, not in love, and content with the fleeting pleasures within his reach. Such is his friend's report.

Despite Bornecque's ingenious line of argument, one should not, perhaps, brush aside Lepelletier's statements as altogether untrue. They have the value of pointing up the very deliberate and conscious character of Verlaine's poetry, of throwing into relief the fact that Verlaine, in composing his work, was infinitely more concerned with the effects to be obtained and the means of expression to be invented than with the authenticity of the disclosures he was making. Not so much because he was a Parnassian, but because he was steeped in Baudelaire and because authenticity was not a poetic virtue in his view. We may be sure that his concern was not to express some experienced anguish, but rather to discover those combinations of words, rhythms, sonorities, and pauses that gave the effect of anguish. That is where his real interest lay.

However, those who endeavor to discover in the *Poèmes saturniens* personal rather than invented elements are not altogether in the wrong. This collection, which is "impassive" in intent, and which pretends to be no more than an aesthetic fiction, is, despite the poet, one long self-revelation. It is such, first of all, because it betrays some of the aspects of sensibility peculiar to Verlaine. We admire, in these poems, exquisitely executed points of craft, subtleties of tone and form. He possessed what was stronger than any outside influence, an innate gift and private preoccupations that had been apparent in the little boy from his earliest years. "The eyes," Verlaine wrote later, "I was precocious, especially, in the eyes. I stared at everything, no aspect of anything escaped me. I was unceasingly on the prowl for shapes, colors, shadows." If this marvelous sensibility is less attracted by bright light, lively colors, and ingenious forms than by subtle nuances and shaded contours, it is because as a very young child Verlaine showed a natural preference for night and its mysteries. "Night," he said, "drew me, a kind of curiosity impelled me to it, I was seeking I know not what— white—gray—shadings perhaps."

The landscapes in *Poèmes saturniens*, the woods, pools, meadows sleeping in the mist, are personally observed and experienced ones. They are the "mournful landscapes" of the Artois district, the Arleux marshlands where the schoolboy had spent his vacations. A letter of 1862 describes them, and all the features it pinpoints are those that reappear in *Poèmes saturniens*: marshlands shaded by poplars and willows, filled with an undergrowth of rushes, white and yellow water lilies; thickets full of shadowy byways where nightingales sing in the evening. Verlainian landscapes are not arbitrary artistic inventions.

But much more than by his confessions, a poet reveals himself in the steady or broken pulsation of his song, in its coloring and its rhythm. Verlaine, indeed, wishing to convey the melancholia of modern times, disciplined his genius to that end. However, in comparing *Poèmes saturniens* with the collections of his masters and friends, one essential and individual element, an element that betrays his secret, emerges from his work. To take but one example: Pierre Martino, in his fine book on Verlaine, compared "Après trois ans" (After Three Years) and Baudelaire's "Je n'ai pas oublié, voisine de la ville . . . ." (I Have Not Forgotten, Neighboring the Town . . . .) The imitation, or at the very least the kinship, is glaring and undisguised —the modest house, the little garden, the weathered plaster statues. In Baudelaire, however, the scene is progressively filled in with resplendent colors. The streaming and magnificent sun sheds its lovely rays upon the humble scene and transfigures it. With Verlaine, on the contrary, the song does not rise. It breaks up, it grows more and more withdrawn, it ends in a murmur. Rejection of joy and hope, mistrust of life, something constricts the throat and chokes off song. If there is any self-disclosure in *Poèmes saturniens*, that is it.

Furthermore, it would perhaps be a mistake to set the theory of impassive art up against the notion of subjectivity. This love of art, in Verlaine, is born precisely of a rejection of life and of any effort to master it. The poet had already said this in "Vers dorés." The great, he had written, are those who have "freed themselves from the yoke of the passions," and who, after fierce battle, have managed to "master life." This attitude, coming as it does from a zealous supporter of impassiveness in art, draws its inspiration from mistrust of men and from a secret horror of life. Verlaine's "ideality," as Lepelletier calls it—his impassiveness—would be inconceivable if he had not, according to his biographer, been ignorant of "those ecstasies, those desires, those joys and those sorrows of first loves" that had, since the beginning of the century, comprised the usual content of first collections by young poets.

In short, this volume, whose intention is wholly impersonal, is in reality the confession of a unique experience. Once the part played by influences and all other borrowed elements has been determined, the essence remains—which is the song of a sorrowful, restless, and wounded soul. Much later, Verlaine spoke of his first volume of verse with admirable judiciousness and subtlety. He emphasized the qualities one might discover in it that already foreshadowed the works to come. He pinpointed, in this early work, tendencies already well established—a substratum of ideas inconsistent in their mixing of dream and reality; a gloominess of thought, "a certain tone flavored with velvet-soft bitterness and cool maliciousness." He admits to the confessional aspect that Lepelletier was later to deny. "The man," he said, "who lay beneath the rather pedantic young man I then was, sometimes threw off or sometimes raised the mask and expressed himself in a number of little poems, tenderly."

In this same essay he drew attention to the already rather free versification, the runovers and enjambments that usually depended on two adjoining caesuras, the frequent alliteration, that something approaching internal assonance, and to the paucity rather than the abundance of rhyme.

Poèmes saturniens was published by Lemerre just before November 17, 1866. Four hundred and ninety-one copies were printed at the author's expense. Very few copies were sold, and twenty years later this modest printing was still not sold out. It has been said that the press maintained an almost total silence. J. H. Bornecque, however, has discovered six articles that mention the new collection. But most of these show an ill will that is as devoid of impartiality as it is of intelligence. The three lines that Barbey d'Aurevilly wrote in *Nain jaune* (Yellow Dwarf) are not, alas, any more distinguished for their fairness. Anatole France wrote a note in the *Chasseur bibliographe* (Bibliographical Inquirer). It testifies to his friendship rather than his insight. He praised the profession of faith in the "Epilogue" and expressed admiration for "César Borgia" and "La Mort de Philippe II" (The Death of Philip II). Verlaine had sent copies to his masters. The responses from Hugo, Leconte de Lisle, Banville, and Sainte-Beuve are painfully banal or ridiculous. Jules de Goncourt admired "Nocturne parisien" (Paris Nocturne). One person only, an unknown poet and humble teacher in Besançon, was capable of writing the right words. His name was Mallarmé.

AFTER POÈMES SATURNIENS

In 1867, after the publication of *Parnasse*, after the polemics of the *Parnassiculet contemporain* (Anthologette of Contemporary Parnassus) and Barbey d'Aurevilly's "Médaillonnets" (Medallionettes), a Parnassian school is in existence, and Verlaine is part of it. We should not assume, however, that Leconte de Lisle's authority is equally recognized by all, and that the group constitutes a solid bloc. One notes around the leader of the school, his ardent disciples—those who, together with Sully-Prudhomme, see in Leconte de Lisle the arbiter of artistic expression, the pride of poetry, the aristocrat of thought—and those, on the other hand, who are more drawn to Baudelaire, who engage in "investigation of the unexplored depths of modern corruption," or who, more simply, require that poetry record the vibrations, complexities, the humble or affecting beauty of "modernity." Among the young Parnassians one distinguishes as well a trend, quite alien to Leconte de Lisle and Mendès, an attempt to garner the interesting elements from realism, to integrate into poetry the useful explorations of Champfleury, the Goncourt brothers, and of certain less well-known novelists. It is from among these diverse elements that Verlaine had to choose.

At one point he paid visits to Leconte de Lisle and figured among the master's disciples at his Sunday morning receptions. But he did not like him. The sardonic manner of the head of the Parnassian school irritated him and was not less wounding to certain others of his alleged disciples. They spoke of his "hideous smile." It is Verlaine who later reported this. One may suppose that he cut a rather sorry figure in a milieu he found so unpleasant. At Leconte de Lisle's, a witness tells us, he took little part in discussion and showed few signs of life. At Lemerre's, with the Parnassian crowd, he was, another witness relates, fidgety and discomfited. He attracted so little attention that Gabriel Marc, in his *Entresol du Parnasse*, forgets to include him in the exact enumeration he makes of the youthful band. Verlaine's real circle is the Hôtel de Ville group of poets. After work, Valade, Mérat, and Armand Renaud meet with him at the Café du Gaz on Rue de Rivoli. Georges Lafenestre goes there, too, and a jovial lawyer, Emile Blémont, whose first book, in 1866, met with a scornful reception from Leconte de Lisle. François Coppée also comes to join forces with this group. The author of *Intimités* lived, as did Verlaine and Blémont, in the Batignolles quarter. This was enough to bring into being the "Batignolles group," a kind of annex to the "Hôtel de Ville poets." There, much more than with the Parnassian school, is where Verlaine's circle lay. Coppée, especially, is his friend at this time. It is Coppée who recommends the manuscript of *Amies* to Poulet-Malassis. Verlaine, in a letter to Hugo of September 1867, speaks of his "good friend Coppée." The following year, it is Verlaine who, in *Hanneton* (May Bug), writes a very thorough and laudatory critique of *Intimités*. This friendship goes so far as to include collaboration. In 1867 the two friends rough out an adaptation of *King Lear* which, however, never gets much beyond that stage. The January 2, 1868, issue of *Hanneton* contains a review, "Qui veut des merveilles?" (Who Wants Wonders?), written jointly by Verlaine and Coppée. Moreover, we observe that Verlaine is a frequent visitor at this period of the Café de Bobino, on Rue de Fleurus, near the Luxembourg garden. He meets there with his friends Coppée, Mérat, and Valade, who are joined by Glatigny whenever he is passing through Paris.

These "Hôtel de Ville" poets are, indeed, Parnassians—but dissenting Parnassians. They willingly contribute to Eugène Vermersch's *Hanneton*. They are oriented toward a poetry of democratic and popular inspiration, or at the very least, toward a realism that we might well call populist. It is Blémont who, in the August 8, 1866, issue of *Nain jaune*, printed his "Sous-maîtresse" (Submistress)—that is, before Coppée's "Crépuscule" (Twilight) in *Poèmes modernes*. One summer evening, Blémont received his friends at home on Rue la Bruyère. He read them his *Confession*, a dramatic monologue, then unpublished and soon after to inspire Coppée to write his "Grève des forgerons" (Strike of the Ironworkers). Coppée, at this date, is determinedly turning toward a poetry that is close to prose, a poetry which shrinks more than anything from appearances of artifice and effort, which turns its back on the funambulatory tricks of the school of fancy. In writing his "Grève des forgerons" he is perfectly aware that he is going against school orthodoxy, and he foresees the indignation it will arouse in the Parnassian group. But he is scornful. "Opinion of the constipated," he writes. Finally, a sense of poetry very close to Coppée's *Intimités* has been rightly observed in the sonnets that Mérat contributed to *Parnasse* in 1866. This poetry comes, for those who can see and feel, out of the most matter-of-fact kind of reality. It has an Ile de France setting, a suburban niche where Parisians drink their Argenteuil and eat their "fish and chips."

This explains the dual orientation evident in the poems Verlaine had written up to that time. "Le Clown," "Intérieur" (Interior), "Circonspection" (Circumspection), which were all printed in *Hanneton* during 1867, make one think of Manet canvases: a vision of a woman in the spell of a cloud of musk and balsam, two silent persons in the calm of night, tense and anguished beings lost in the hostile mob. Certain prose pieces of the same period—"Le Corbillard" (The Hearse), and "Mal'aria" (Evil Melody)—are in the same mode: a graphic and perceptive modernity with the note of sadness that is his trademark. One is reminded of the article in which Verlaine praised the poetic qualities of Coppée's recent volume: "exquisite, extremely subtle lines, which seem effortless, which even slightly affect an elegiac casualness, mocked at times by a light note of somber irony . . . ."

At the same time, however, Verlaine's "Les Loups" (The Wolves) and "Le Soldat laboureur" (The Farmer Soldier) were being published in the *Revue des lettres et des arts*; "Les Poètes," later titled "Les Vaincus" (The Vanquished), in *La Gazette rimée*; and "Le Monstre" (The Monster) in *Nain jaune*. Here, no more little scenes à la Mérat, no more exquisite and gloomy emotions. But rather a plain, rough language, the epic style of Hugo's people's poetry. A whole realist vein that was not soon to run out. In 1869, Verlaine was working on "L'Angelus du Matin" (Morning Angelus) and "La Soupe du soir" (Evening Meal). And preparing, with Lepelletier, an ambitious popular play, *Les Forgerons* (The Ironworkers), on which they worked very hard during August 1869. He decided to submit several of these pieces for publication in the second volume of *Parnasse*, and the reading committee accepted them.

This has astonished many critics. They cannot accept the idea that Verlaine, at the very time he was writing *Fêtes galantes* (Love's Revels), was composing poems of such a different sort. This is apparently because they have formed too rigid and incomplete an idea of the poet. Verlaine took a lively interest in the progress of realism. He was not at all scornful of the unfashionable and unsuccessful efforts of Champfleury; so Lepelletier has reported. He admired, says this biographer, not only Balzac's novels, but such obscure works as *Antoine Quérard* by Charles Bataille and Ernest Rasetti. He followed the work of the Goncourt brothers with sympathy and attention, and one may be sure that he was among those who clapped loudest at the performance of *Henriette Maréchal*.

These interests, which critics have neglected, can be explained. Many good minds had grown weary of the purely gratuitous kind of art that the Art for Art's Sake school had for a long time now chosen to support. They wanted a return to seriousness, to the real, or, as some said, to "life." It is interesting to note that Banville himself felt this need. "We are all," he wrote, "so satiated with every possible kind of jugglery that we can no longer be touched except by real-life poetry." Thus the poets came to adopt certain Barbey d'Aurevilly's theses. He had, in the name of "life," denounced the sterility of the Art for Art's Sake school: "Cheap exercise in rhyming, tricks of versification, straddling verses, *ronds de jambes de danseuse*." We may be certain that Verlaine followed attentively the polemics of a man whose views he found questionable but whom he admired.

To use an expression unknown to that epoch, Verlaine viewed the idea of an "engaged" poetry without qualms. His revolutionary convictions, his opposition to the Empire, his Hébertist principles, inspired him to write poems meant to destroy tyranny. "Les Loups" is a symbolic piece. It tells of the haughty triumph of the winning faction over the unfortunate heroes of the popular cause. Verlaine had already known those brutish and dastardly hearts, at once grasping and cowardly, in the magistrates of the Empire and in the venal publicists who denounced, censured, and persecuted the remains of the Republican party. The poem "Les Vaincus" is in a similar vein. In its original form, and with its old title, "Les Poètes," it expresses the helpless anger of the survivors of the people's revolution. The ideal, the dream of brotherhood, is dead. Realpolitik triumphs. Those who have escaped the repression—hunted, discouraged—have believed everything finished. But the Empire is showing signs of shakiness:

> *Une faible lueur palpite à l'horizon.*

> A feeble light flickers on the horizon.

The end of the poem, in the form it took in 1867, is a call to resume the great battle once more. It has been said that the title, "Les Poètes," proves the absence of any political intent. This is to forget that since Pierre Leroux there had been a continuing tradition that assigned to poets the obligation to sound the call to freedom.

To these works of open or concealed revolutionary inspiration are aligned purely descriptive pieces that are merely popular in character. "Le Soldat laboureur" is both a sympathetic and amused evocation of the survivors of the Grand Army. "La Soupe du soir" is a touching picture of working-class poverty. To interpret these pieces properly, one should compare them to the poems François Coppée was composing during the same period, poems that were later to make up his *Poésies modernes*, i.e., "Angelus," "Le Père" (The Father), "Saragosse" (Saragossa), and "La Grève des forgerons."

Verlaine had undertaken the composition of a volume in this mode. He had given it the overall title of *Les Vaincus*. He was working on it in April of 1869 and expressed impatience the following August at the slowness of its execution. To his mind, this book was to serve as a counterpart to *Fêtes galantes*, its strength balancing the gracefulness of the other. Critics are generally very scornful of this portion of his work. They forget that in 1873, when he had just finished the most exquisite of his collections, *Romances sans paroles* (Songs without Words), the poet stubbornly returned to this project. They do not see that this poetry, oriented as it is to real life, heralds the subsequent development of the writer and indicates the path he will follow. This will no longer be the path of service to the cause of freedom, but rather that of service to man in the form of the converted poet's notion of truth and salvation. To turn one's back on juvenile games, acrobatic feats of prosody, gratuitous artifice, to give poetry a concrete meaning, to make the poet the interpreter of our passions and of our hopes, is not necessarily a wrong thing to do.

In a wholly different vein Verlaine composed, in 1867 at the latest, a series of six sonnets entitled *Les Amies* (Girl Friends), inspired by Baudelaire's *Femmes damnées*. His friend Coppée brought them to the attention of Poulet-Malassis in Belgium, who undertook to have them printed. They were attributed to the licentious writer, Pablo-Maria de Herlagnez. This work, which was deemed scandalous, was intercepted at the French border. Only a few copies escaped seizure. Nothing shows better than *Les Amies* the difference between Baudelaire's and Verlaine's vision. The sapphic poems of the former are imbued with an atmosphere heavy with sensuous odors and take place in a shadowy world in which the rites of an age-old and mysterious cult are enacted. *Les Amies* speaks of the passionate urgings of sensual desire and evokes a picture of young and supple bodies, blue eyes, and white muslin curtains. Verlaine attempts in vain to imitate Baudelaire, speaks in vain of the glorious stigma, of the noble vow of these sublime damned souls. The key signature—and the tempo —remain profoundly different.

FÊTES GALANTES

Side by side with *Les Vaincus*, Verlaine was preparing another collection of fanciful and *art pur* poetry. He had chosen the "revels of love" as a theme. He had, as early as 1867, contributed two pieces on this theme to *La Gazette rimée*. The following year he had six others printed in *L'Artiste*.

Early in the winter of 1868–1869, he was taken to Nina de Callias' salon. She was twenty-five years old. She had been married at one time, but had been divorced since 1867. She was an excellent musician and had been one of the first in France to appreciate Wagner. To be seen at her house were Charles Cros and Villiers de l'Isle-Adam, Anatole France, Dierx, Valade, Coppée—Verlaine's best friends. He was delighted. He held no small position in Nina's salon: the habitués inflicted on him the nickname Gwinplaine.

This intelligent and freeminded group pretended to a kind of sharp-edged modernity à la Baudelaire. Nina, a very dark-complexioned woman, presided, some outlandish ornament in her hair, wrapped in a Japanese robe. They talked in slang. Wagner was worshiped, Offenbach doted on. In a poem written in July 1869, Verlaine wrote:

> *Dieux, quel hiver*
> *Nous passâmes! Ce fut amer*
> *Et doux. Un sabbat! une fête!*

> Heavens, what a winter
> We spent! It was bitter
> And sweet. A Sabbath! A revel!

It was not Nina's soirées that inspired *Fêtes galantes*, for the collection had been started a year earlier. One would like to think, however, that the frenzied drive of certain poems reflects the feverish atmosphere of those "bitter and sweet" revels.

Eighteenth century France was once more in style. The poets had done much to recover the beauty of that most elegant and refined of periods. Gautier had written "Rocaille," "Pastel," "Watteau," and his marvelous "Carnaval de Venise." Banville's *En Habit zinzolin* (In Violet Attire) had been published. Hugo had costumed the characters of *La Fête chez Thérèse* (The Party at Theresa's) in Watteau style. A very short time before, *Les Chansons des rues et des bois* (Songs of the Streets and Forests) had included a piece, "La Lettre," which was very similar to Verlaine's *Fêtes galantes*. Thanks to these masters, the young Parnassians had learned to appreciate the poetry of an earlier, now defunct society. Mendès was writing his *Traversée galante* (Love Voyage) and his "Sonnet dans le goût ancien" (Sonnet in the Style of Former Days). In his *Flèches d'Or* (Golden Arrows) Glatigny evoked the "lovely gallant shades" in the groves they had once haunted. He dreamed of seeing once again that sweet fairyland, that French Walpurgis-time which bourgeois insipidity had disrupted.

One name had become the symbol of the poetic and gallant eighteenth century, that of Watteau—and history should not forget the pilgrimage that Arsène Houssaye, Philippe Burty, Charles Coligny, and other admirers of the painter made to Nogent-sur-Marne in 1865. *L'Artiste,* one of the most widely read magazines of the literary world, gave an account of it and reprinted Arsène Houssaye's speech.

Watteau's work at this date, however, was difficult to know well. The Louvre had only his "L'Embarquement pour Cythère." His other paintings belonged to private collections and remained inaccessible. However, fine research work by J. H. Bornecque has drawn attention to several volumes wherein the art appreciator of the period might study Watteau's work. They were Charles Blanc's *Les Peintres des Fêtes Galantes* (The Painters of Love's Revels), published in 1854, and, especially, a volume containing forty-three reproductions published under the title: *Pièces choisies composées par A. Watteau et gravées*

par W. *Marks. Tirées de la collection de* M.A. *Dinaux,* 1850
(A Selection of Works Painted by A. Watteau and Engraved
by W. Marks. Chosen from the M. A. Dinaux Collection, 1850).
Thus the Goncourt brothers were not the first or the only people
to make Watteau appreciated and admired. At any rate, however, their study, published in 1860, is one of the most likely
sources of Verlaine's book. One of the best writers on *Fêtes
galantes*—Ernest Dupuy—has contrasted the vital and distinct
charm of the eighteenth century with the casual and rather
vagrant characters in Verlaine. His characters bring Shakespeare's fairy creatures to mind. The Goncourt brothers, however, were unaware of this contrast. "In some random place not
to be found on the map of the earth, there is," they said, "an
unceasing indolence under the trees. . . . A Lethe prevails over
the silence in this land of forgetfulness, which is peopled with
shapes that have eyes and mouths only: a burning and a smile."
They themselves conjured up Shakespeare and his love comedies. The interpretation of Watteau in Verlaine's *Fêtes galantes*
was that of the Goncourts before him. As did his masters, the
young poet heard, underlying the merry banterings, the murmur
of a slow and indistinct music. He detected the melodious and
mildly contagious sadness they conceal. It would be hard to
prove this interpretation false. At most one might point out
that it throws emphasis on the melancholy and dark side of
this admirable work—and makes its joy, translucence, and its
impulse toward happiness less conspicuous.

Like Ernest Dupuy, but for more numerous and more specific
reasons, J. H. Bornecque stresses the inexactitude of the *Fêtes
galantes*, the romantic distortion the poems impose on Watteau's work. He points out that only one out of a hundred of
the paintings has a fountain in it. In his view, Verlaine's interpretation of the dark side of Watteau's work comes from Glatigny and Banville; and the enchanted setting of the first sonnet
—its waterfalls, its fountains among the trees—comes from one
of Charles Blanc's pages. All of these observations are valuable.
But is there any reason why Verlaine should not have known
the paintings of Hubert Robert, his marble steps, his flights of
stairs, his fountains? And why, above all, should we wish to see
Verlaine's *Fêtes galantes* as a mere gloss of Watteau?

The *fêtes* are, first of all, a revivification of the fairy-tale
fancies of the Italian Commedia. The subject was in fashion.
Maurice Sand had published, in 1859, a thick book of *Masques
et Bouffons* (Masks and Buffoons). *The Revue des deux mondes*
had recently devoted several articles to the Commedia dell' Arte.
Lataye's article in the December 1859 issue had, for instance,
stressed the appeal to the imagination, the chimerical poetry
of this art form. Around it, he said, gathered the restless minds,
the souls discontented with reality, the poets, musicians, painters
who can fulfill themselves only in dreams and hallucinations.

If Maurice Sand's book had drawn attention to the subject,
Verlaine might also have found sources of earlier date elsewhere.
In "Carnaval de Venise," Gautier had summoned up Doctor
Bolognese, Scaramouche, Punchinello—and Banville, in his
Odes funambulesques (Funambulatory Odes) had dealt with
the same subject in "Folies nouvelles" (New Madnesses). The
influence of these authors is readily visible in *Fêtes galantes* and
enables one to understand its details. The Pierrot in "Panto-
mime" is clearly Banville's in his "Folies nouvelles." Lazy and
greedy, he owes very little to Watteau.

Certain of the *Fêtes galantes* make one think more of Voiture
and of Benserade than of the painter of "L'Embarquement
pour Cythère." These two men, poets par excellence in the
mannered polite style, had just emerged from long and un-
merited oblivion. Catulle Mendès mentioned Benserade in his
work, and Glatigny quoted him in "Nocturne." One whole
portion of *Fêtes galantes* takes its inspiration from this redis-
covered preciosity: "A la Promenade" (Walking), "Dans la
Grotte" (In the Grotto), "Mandoline" (Mandolin), "Lettre"
(Letter). These poems, which have no reference to Watteau,
have the common feature of avoiding expressions of tender love
and languidness, and of seeing love as a lively, ironical, and
slightly licentious mental game. The men are deceivers and
charming, the women coquettes who, if they become annoyed
by uncalled-for liberties, do so with a smile. These Clymènes
play out the subtle comedies of love with their Tircises and
their Clitandres. They feign cruelty. They mime despair with
the same unserious grandiloquence as the mocking lovers of
Ismene and Amarante in Banville, and they cultivate the same

precious metaphoric turn of speech that Glatigny had so wittily parodied in a recent work.

The more one studies *Fêtes galantes*, the clearer it becomes that it is impossible to explain the book by the Watteau interpretation. It is rather of Fragonard that we are often reminded—of the eighteenth century of freethinking clerics and of Camargo, the dancer who once upon a time had Paris at her feet. It is vain to insist that "Sur l'Herbe" (On the Grass) was inspired by Watteau's "Assemblée dans un parc" (Gathering in a Park), or by his "Divertissements champêtres" (Country Diversions). It finds its source in the frenzied Musset of "Les Marrons du feu" (Flaming Chestnuts), and the straying cleric might well be our old friend, Annibal Desiderio. Similarly, "En Bateau" (Boating), in which one recognizes a vein that had at an earlier time inspired Banville's "L'Arbre de Judée" (The Judas Tree) and certain lines of "En Habit zinzolin."

Sometimes it is to still another painter we must turn. "Les Ingénus" seems to be a commentary on some lines by the Goncourt brothers on Greuze's women. They had spoken of their innocence as "facile and on the brink of being lost," of their *ingenuousness*—that of Cécile de Volanges, for instance —as "a powerless and unexamined ingenuousness, susceptible to surprise, the senses, and to pleasure." Following Mendès' example, Verlaine discerned this feature and was inspired by it.

He had been under the spell of the poetic mode of *Fêtes galantes* since 1866. In *Poèmes saturniens*, "La Nuit du Walpurgis classique" (Classical Walpurgis Night), which was inspired by Glatigny, already augurs the collection to come. The stanzas that were to serve him as a transition to *Fêtes galantes* and a poem titled "Trumeau" (Trollop), later "Mandoline," appeared in *La Gazette rimée* of February 20, 1867. In the middle of the same year, he contributed "Paysage historique" (Historical Scene) to *Hanneton*. This latter poem was not included in his book. It would not, however, have been too out of place. It is a brief meditation on an old tapestry. It becomes quite emotional about this simple and mawkish, this trite and artificial subject. One finds some of this deliberate naïveté and mawkishness in certain of the poems in *Fêtes galantes*.

This slim volume was a marvelous success. People did not

find, as they had in *Poèmes saturniens,* lack of assimilation of borrowed elements. From all indications given by the Goncourts, Gautier, Banville, Glatigny, and Mendès, the poet had created an admirably unified work. Beneath a pale sky in which a pink and hazy moon is drifting, the characters of the *Fêtes galantes* and of the Italian Commedia pass in groups. Slender trees throw soft blue shadows on them. A landscape takes shape, the pure invention of the poet, the plastic expression of his imagination. And among the groves, the marble pools, and the fountains, beings sing and laugh. They pretend to be gay, a little mad, abandoned to pleasure. But on close examination one detects an uneasiness about them. They fear passion and their weaknesses. They know that love play ends badly, that love is an illusion, and that a sardonic and evil fate hovers over the life of men. The terracotta faun is the symbol of this fate, and the pilgrims of life have no hope of escaping it.

This poetry of an all-embracing melancholy dimension is, however, meant to be a game. For illusion is regent of the world, and it is for the most intelligent not to be taken in. The poet amuses himself. He amuses himself with the relationships in "A Clymène": Baudelaire's sober doctrine here becomes a pretext for subtle combinations of hues and fragrances. The enjambments that set off the ironical charge of a phrase, and the rhymes—profuse, unusual, employed in a hundred original ways—these are part of the fun.

Fêtes galantes already proclaims the idea that poetry is, above all, music. Verlaine multiplies the number of internal assonances and alliterations. These are deliberately muted, sliding, drawn-out. He places them, it seems, at random—but, actually, with a view to avoiding symmetrical recurrences. *Fêtes galantes* is a song, the song that Verlaine heard within himself during the best moments of his life.

These explorations of sound and rhythm led Verlaine in a direction in which he was later to engage himself fully. In reading "L'Allée" (The Walk), one observes that the sentence structure is extended, richly, supplely, turns back on itself, resists set constructions and symmetrical arrangement. Some poems already show a taste for broken meters. "En Patinant" (While Skating) contains one line,

> *Mais que d'une façon moins noire!*
> But in how less somber a way!

which foreshadows the future liberties of Verlaine's language.

Our age, which is both barbarous and pedantic, in which bombast and upheaval triumph, is ill-prepared to appreciate the delicate beauties of this music and this poetry. He who would appreciate its perfections might take note of the setting that Claude Debussy gave to "Les Ingénus." The charming melody that the poem inspired him to write is closely modelled on Verlaine's meters, on the weight of each of the syllables. First we hear the quick movement of a walk but little slowed by shoes that are too high-heeled and long, full skirts. It is the sound of sport, of laughter, a very quick and halting tempo. Then the rhythm changes. From drawn-out and muted syllables there emerges an impression of languor, unexpressed emotion, gentle resignation. The shadow of unending illusion falls upon the formerly joyous and noisy couples.

Three hundred and fifty copies of *Fêtes galantes* were printed. The printing was finished on February 20, 1869, and the publicity on the book was done in the weeks that followed. Banville reviewed it in the April 19 *National*. On April 16, Hugo sent a note of praise from Guernsey. Lepelletier promised to do an article, but it was never written. Silence fell on this unpretentious and audacious work, and on the revelation it contained.

LA BONNE CHANSON (SONG OF THE GOOD)

Fêtes galantes had barely been published when Verlaine met Mathilde. His engagement inspired a number of poems which he brought together in the volume that comprises his *Song of the Good*.

In their disagreement over the value of this collection and over the place it occupies in the history of Verlaine's body of work, the critics have shown how difficult it is to judge it properly. Some do not conceal how little value they place on this overly discreet, quite flavorless and fragile poetry that is the work of a young bourgeois who is settling down. As P. Martino wittily puts it, this nice young educated man would cut a fine figure in a Theuriet novel, on the arm of a highly Second Empire young lady. Others, however, admire the collection as a definite step forward—as a break with *Parnasse* and as Verlaine's accession to the kind of poetry for which he was born, the poetry of artless sincerity and total spontaneity. Edmond Lepelletier is not, by far, as warm in his praises. But he agrees in seeing in *La Bonne Chanson* the emergence of a "new poetics." Verlaine, in his view, shifts from objective, descriptive, concrete poetry to a poetry of confession, of recording the pulsations of the heart. And he, too, adjudges this step decisive.

Although positive proof may be lacking, one may well believe that Verlaine wanted to break with *artisterie*, as he was to call it a few years later. Because he was resolved to become a solid middle-class person, because he was settling down, he shifted his sights, and he decided to avoid the all too obvious artifices in which certain of the Parnassians saw the essence of poetry. He went directly to the unadulterated springs of inspiration, to the very simple, very human feelings that were at that time in his life responsible for his happiness.

This dream of spontaneous poetry, however, is altogether illusory. No poetry is spontaneous. Let us not imagine that beneath the inspiration of *Fêtes galantes*, which is entirely dominated by artistic concerns, lay another deeper, purer vein. Let us rather say that from this time on there appear in Verlaine's work—linked with his efforts toward a stricter moral life—certain special ways of thinking and feeling, certain distinctive modes of expression. These may be seen even now in *La Bonne Chanson*. They will reappear later—in the poems of lesser quality—in *Sagesse* (Wisdom).

Far from marking a return to the pure springs of inspiration, these seemingly spontaneous works are the result of an effort of man's least poetic faculties—of the concept-building intellect, of the will affecting lofty attitudes. Abstract words abound, often made to stand out by use of capital letters. Mathilde is the Partner, she is Hope. Impure Doubt is put to flight, and the World is vanquished. The poet is terrified by suspicion, doubt, and apprehension, which cast shadows over love. Adjectives are no longer used to convey subtle nuances, but rather to delineate the idea of the poem, to mark its contours, to make it stand out in its essential and icy purity. The soul is noble, the heart virtuous. Verlaine advances straight and calmly down treacherous roads, he confronts sensual pleasures, he aspires to the austere ecstasy of the upright man. These epithets, to say the least, bring nothing surprising or subtle to the poem. Once settled upon the path of pure intellect, Verlaine is content with general maxims. Whence his very curious use of the pronoun *one* in song X, a usage that will recur in *Sagesse*. His shortcomings, his good resolutions, are the shortcomings and resolutions of all men. This allegedly personal poetry verges on willful banality.

However, the most unquestionable failing of *La Bonne Chanson* in a number of its parts, the failing that absolutely prevents one's seeing in it any definite advance over *Fêtes galantes* and that even forces one to say that Verlaine has gone astray, is that this new collection too often assumes that poetry depends, not on transposition, that sustained "metaphor" which is the essence of art, but on the direct statement, as content, of his feelings. Thus it is not by imagery, nor by the music of words, nor by rhythmic phrasing that Verlaine conveys to us the joy with which he is filled. He *states* it, just as those who are not poets state it. He explains, he enumerates his reasons for fearing and hoping. He speaks to our intellect. He leaves nothing to our imagination.

Other poems, however, strike a note of genuine poetry. Some of these are "intimacies," subtly and authentically scored: a portrait of Mathilde seated at her sister's side, a cozy apartment at teatime, a suburban street, a group of plane trees losing their leaves, a horsecar in a din of clanking iron. Two poems, in short, V and VI, are genuine songs. In them the poet does not attempt to express lofty thoughts. He does not tell us he is full of joy. But the quails in the thyme, the larks in the sky, the dew that glitters brightly on the hay convey his joy.

In the spring of 1870, he put these poems together in a book, discarding only three that were a little too highly spiced. Printing was finished on June 12. The edition ran to five hundred and ninety copies. A number of these were sent to mentors and friends. Hugo thanked him. Banville wrote the article that Verlaine hoped for. But the war had just broken out. Release for sale was postponed. The volume was not announced in

Bibliographie de la France until December 3, and it was not until 1872 that it appeared in the bookstore windows. Sales were practically nil.

ROMANCES SANS PAROLES (SONGS WITHOUT WORDS)

The war, and to an even greater extent, the Commune, had broken up the Parnassian group. Leconte de Lisle and his followers raged at the defeated faction. Mérat, Lepelletier, Blémont, and Valade were up in arms over the dreadful repressive measures. The split was definitive, and a few conciliatory gestures should not lead us to think otherwise. The Parnassian school, truncated, deprived of its best elements, had all it could do to survive. For those who had shared in the hopes of the Parisian revolt, or who at least had experienced the excesses of the reaction to it, it was a question of regrouping. Beginning in the first half of August 1871, they revived the dinner meetings of the Vilains Bonshommes. Verlaine, naturally, was one of them. There he once again met his prewar friends and a number of new members—Jean Aicard, Ernest d'Hervilly, and Pierre Elzéar. In April 1872, Emile Blémont founded, together with Jean Aicard, Elzéar, and Valade, a magazine called *La Renaissance littéraire et artistique.* Verlaine, too, was among the contributors.

It was in this group that he had his friendships, his sympathies, his ties. Coppée and France had broken with him. Leconte de Lisle speaks of him only to express surprise that he has not yet been shot. His break with *Parnasse*, then, was total and showed itself in his personal relationships even before it was made articulate in his poetic theory.

In Blémont's group, one word inspires the poets: life. They feel strongly about the artificial, frigid, and inhuman aspects of Parnassian orthodoxy. Soon the group of "The Living"— "les Vivants"—will be formed. The name is already appropriate to the contributors to *Renaissance.* Poetry, in their view, should express modern life, seized in its graphic aspects, or tapped at its source in the contemporary soul—that troubled, restless soul—torn between yearnings after the ideal and the attractions of the flesh. The poems in *Romances sans paroles* become clear once one has seen them in the perspective of the workings of this amicable group.

The book was not published until March 1874, but this date should not mislead us. The selections that comprise the collection were written from the beginning of 1872 up through the first months of 1873. They are properly explained only through an investigation of the circumstances in which they were composed.

The group of "Ariettes oubliées" (Forgotten Ariettas) make up the first part of the book. The first poem appeared in the May 18, 1872, issue of *Renaissance*, the second was sent to Blémont in a letter dated September, the fifth is included in the June 29 issue of *Renaissance*, and the ninth and last poem bears the date May-June 1872. These factual details have more than chronological interest. They enable one to grasp the underlying purpose of the poems.

The first months of 1872 were marked by an attempt on Verlaine's part to recapture Mathilde's heart, to erase the horrible memory of the previous few months. He was alone in Paris from the second half of January to the middle of March. He wrote Mathilde letters we no longer have, but which we do know begged her to return. Most of the *ariettes* were written at this time and during the weeks that followed her return.

From this one may explain these lines in the first *ariette:*

> *Cette âme qui se lamente*
> *En cette plainte dormante,*
> *C'est la nôtre, n'est-ce pas?*
> *La mienne, dis et la tienne . . .*

> This soul that makes its lament
> In this somnolent complaint,
> Is ours, is it not?
> Mine, say, and yours . . .

The second, titled "Escarpolette" (Swing), is an expression of Verlaine's wavering between lawful love and forbidden love, the distraction of a delirious heart—and the "dear love that takes fright" is Mathilde, who has fled, terrified, to Périgueux.

It has been supposed that the fourth *ariette* was addressed to Rimbaud, and that Verlaine was thinking of Rimbaud when he wrote:

> *Soyons deux enfants, soyons deux jeunes filles.*

> Let's be two children, let's be two young girls.

But does not the allusion in the last verse refer to the anticipated reconciliation, seeing that the two children are going once again to walk beneath chaste arbors

> *Sans même savoir qu'elles sont pardonnées.*

> Without even knowing they are forgiven.

The fifth *ariette* is, if possible, clearer still. Mathilde has left. Verlaine dreams of the little bower on Rue Nicolet where her scent still lingers in the air, and of the little garden that separates the house from the roadway.

The eighth *ariette* is perhaps the earliest of the group and is explained by the trip Verlaine made to Paliseul at the end of December 1871. It was snowing, and the poet, according to Delahaye, was recalling the long route over the frozen landscape when he wrote in *Sagesse:*

> *Un rêve de froid: que c'est beau, la neige!*

> A dream of cold: how beautiful the snow!

The same occasion may well be taken as the basis of this *ariette* too.

The seventh comes after Mathilde's flight in July. It describes his inconsolable shock, his refusal to believe the break final. It is possible that the third was written in London, sometime in October.

This cycle of "Ariettes oubliées," so clearly defined in time and by the poet's intentions, reveals his desire to make a pure music out of poetry. The title itself is full of significance. It has been said that Rimbaud had written an *ariette oubliée*; this is an error. The truth is that Rimbaud was very fond of Favart's librettos and music. He sent a volume of them to Verlaine from Charleville, and the Mautées found, among the objects left behind by their son-in-law, "a collection of eighteenth century compositions, among others 'Ninette à la Cour' (Ninette at Court) by Favart." Verlaine, who liked old tapestries and eighteenth century painting—even its rather mawkish and old-fashioned qualities—must have enjoyed Favart's music. He had it played for him. Two lines in an arietta from "Ninette," two lines of no special beauty, but which he found affecting, inspired him to write at least the first of his *ariettes*.

Perhaps no other of Verlaine's collections so fully satisfies the requirement that Mallarmé would one day set for poetry—that the poet's duty is to suggest. In contrast to *La Bonne Chanson*, the *ariettes* never *state*, but by means of images, sounds, and rhythms, they make us participate in the deep sorrow of the deserted poet. Let us only look at the first, for example. The spiritual state that Verlaine wishes to convey is that of an almost mute sadness, one that only moans deep within. A sadness that is almost sweet, so many tender images are mingled with it. There is something poignant about it, too, however, for the betrayed man feels very lonely and very helpless. And then the images flash: a slumbering plain, slender trees that tremble in a bitter wind, the soft cry of waving grass. A quivering landscape that grips the heart. A love-filled weariness and languor. Verlaine does not link these images structurally, and because he does not dare go even further and leave out the verb in his sentences, he uses over and over the most insignificant, the most colorless, the least active of all verbs—the verb *to be*. The language becomes more economical, unadorned. It ignores grammatical requirements in order to achieve an extreme humbleness, a baldness that comes as close as anything can to silence. "*C'est* tous les frissons des bois . . ." (*It's* all the quiverings of the woods . . .) he writes, and the wind-tossed grass "emits" its soft cry.

The sounds are selected to give an effect of taut languidness. The rhymes especially: in each stanza there are four lines with feminine rhymes and only two with masculine rhymes. Within the lines, recurrences—the shivery *i*'s of the first stanza, the protracted *u* of *ramures* prefiguring the rhymes in the following stanza. Alliterations that give the gloomy landscape a more cheerful note,

> O le frêle et frais murmure . . .
>
> O the frail and fresh murmur . . .

or, in contrast, the crushing repetitions:

> Les roulis sourd des cailloux.
>
> The muffled rumbling of the pebbles.

Finally, he uses a seven-syllable line. Verlaine in 1872 is fully aware of the musical and suggestive value of uneven meters. He knows that to express the humble, sorry miseries of his life they carry a force quite different from the octosyllabics and alexandrines that are the rule in contemporary poetry.

"Escarpolette" carries this conception of poetic creation to the limit. The swing is for Verlaine the symbol of his life, swinging back and forth between Mathilde and Rimbaud, between tranquil virtue and adventure. This swinging brings on nausea and dizziness. His vision is blurred. In this disordered state he no longer hears one clear, pure voice, but the arietta of all lyres together, the song of the good *and* of the bad. He would like to choose, to settle on one. He cannot, and feels so weary he wants to die. Die far from Mathilde and Rimbaud. Die alone.

More here than in the first of the *ariettes*, Verlaine fixes upon "connections" that mix and confuse the impressions conveyed. V*oices* of the past have *contour*, and the *glimmerings* that herald the future are *musical*. Here this skillful artistry is more than gratuitous play, as it is in *Fêtes galantes*. It is a reflection of the confusion into which Verlaine is plunged at the moment. All the rhymes are feminine, and the music of the words is more complex, reveals intentions more subtle than ever.

Feminine rhyme and broken meter are two obvious features of the "Ariettes oubliées." In this group of nine poems, one finds lines of five, seven, nine, and eleven syllables. Four of them, nearly half, have feminine rhymes exclusively. One of the others presents a curious peculiarity. Verlaine amuses himself by making one masculine syllable rhyme with a feminine syllable: *Jean de Nivelle* with *Michel, robe bleue* with *palsembleu.* It is easy to see his intent. This poem, different from the others in subject, conjures up figures from legend and popular song— Mére Michel and Lustucru, Jean de Nivelle and Jean des Bas-

Bleus. It is the only surviving piece of a series that, according to the poet's plans in November 1872, was meant to make up one of the four sections of the collection, and which was to be titled "Nuit falote" (Quaint Night). It should be noted that Verlaine could have read in Banville's *Stalactites* (Stalactites) an "Elégie" in which *confus* was rhymed with *touffues* and *rochers* with *cachées*.

On July 7, 1872, Verlaine left Mathilde. He crossed the Belgian border near Bouillon. He made his way to Brussels. He stayed in Belgium until September 7. These two months inspired the "Paysages belges" (Belgian Landscapes) series. They follow the stages of his route—Walcourt, Charleroi, Brussels—not omitting an outing to Malines.

We should not look for allusions to his state of mind in these poems. He is concerned solely with graphic notations on the Belgian capital and on the countryside he traverses. No one would suspect in reading them that he was in the midst of living out a tragic experience in which his love and happiness were at stake. These short, purely pictorial pieces merit close attention. In them Verlaine is attempting a very original kind of art, a descriptive style previously unknown.

It has been said that a number of these poems constitute "a strongly impressionist poetry in the sense that the word would acquire fifteen years later in painting." The relationship is unquestionably much more close and specific. The Impressionist revolution took place between 1870 and 1874. Manet changed his style in 1869–1870. In 1870 Monet and Pissarro made their trip to London. In 1871 Cézanne was working in L'Estaque. Dégas, Renoir, Fantin-Latour came on the scene in succession. The group's first exhibition took place in 1874. One of Monet's canvases, "Impression," gave the new school its name, which was meant to be pejorative, of Impressionist. Verlaine met Manet at Nina de Callias' salon. He saw Fantin-Latour daily for the portrait the painter was doing of the editors of *Renaissance*. Through them, through Forain, who was then his daily companion, and through André Gill, he became aware of the ideas fermenting among young painters. He was won over.

It is truly a matter of a new and important achievement in the development of his work. Read, for instance, "Walcourt."

Not one verb, not one regularly constructed sentence. Not one transition. A succession of brief notations, within a luminous and cheerful tonal key. Like the Impressionists, Verlaine paints with pure light, concerned now entirely in rendering the marvelous play and vibration of light. Like them too, he ignores contour, boldly juxtaposes tones. The two techniques correspond. The aesthetic of the ephemeral, Jules Laforgue called impressionism. Verlaine's poetry concentrates on recording the transitory features of a landscape in a moment of light. Brussels is seen on a summer evening, at the hour when the sun hits the tops of the trees horizontally, when the hillside houses and gardens loom up vaguely in a pale pink and green light, like the light through a lampshade. The essential thing for the poet-painter is not to impose arrangements—to repel the intervention of the intellect which orders, and consequently, falsifies and distorts—but rather artlessly to collect impressions, capture them in their natural freshness. "Malines," which is about a train ride is, except at the very end, a marvelous demonstration of this.

If one has any hesitation about accepting the fact that Verlaine was, at the time of "Paysages belges," quite preoccupied with the concerns of impressionism, one should read the notes he took a few weeks later on arriving in London, notes he sent to Blémont and Lepelletier: the outline for a book of *Croquis londiniens* (London Sketches) he hoped one day to publish. One observes in them a very serious effort to discover, beneath its often crude exterior, the hidden poetry of a large modern city. A slow attempt, punctuated by partial revelations and an admitted lack of knowledge. "It is likely," he wrote, "that English life has qualities of poetry still imperceptible to me." And again, in October: "Up until now, although I have seen a good deal here and in the surrounding areas, I perceive none of the poetry of this country, which, I am certain, does not lack it." Like the Impressionists, he is concerned with modern life, with the poetry of the docks, of the Babylonian bridges across the Thames, of the railroad stations. He is reacting against academicism and the jaded beauties "of Italies, Spains, and countries beyond the Rhine." After describing the "endless docks," he adds this observation: "[They] satisfy, moreover, my more and more modernist poetic." After visiting the museums, he notes, disillusioned: "No modernity." These preoccupations, this desire to "collect impressions," this effort to discover the poetry concealed in the heart of things, this is what explains the "Paysages belges" and what makes Verlaine, at this date, the poet of impressionism.

"Birds in the Night" is a separate series in itself. It is likely that Verlaine took the title from a cradlesong Sir Arthur Sullivan had just published. He was the most famous composer of the time, and it is highly probable that Verlaine knew his name and this title. The first three parts of the poem were sent to Blémont on October 5, 1872. On the basis of the images, the words, and the tone alone, "Birds in the Night" is directly related to *La Bonne Chanson,* of which it is the pitiful epilogue or, if one prefers, the obverse, *La Mauvaise Chanson* (Bad Song), as Verlaine called it. The same sort of metaphors: the good fight to fight, the defeated and wounded soldier. The same capital letters: my Beautiful, my Dear. The same adjectives: pure forgiveness, exquisite pitfalls. A whole unreal and childish world. And, as in *La Bonne Chanson,* a tendency to verge on prose, to speak in an undertone, in the plainest and most simple accents.

One might well find these qualities uninviting. One might well feel, too, a little ill at ease in the face of this unreal purity that corresponds so little to all we now know about Verlaine's follies. The interest, however, the very great beauty of "Birds in the Night," lies in the music of the lines. Verlaine wrote this poem in decasyllabics, but rather than breaking at the fourth or sixth syllable, he most often broke after the fifth, an altogether uncommon practice that makes each of his decasyllabic lines a pair of lines of five syllables each. The result is an irregular meter, broken and weary sounding. Quiet reproaches, hopeless grief. A poetry devoid of all rhetoric, all translucent quality, a poetry of pure spirituality. Full of pitfalls to be sure, which are already apparent. For the time being, however, the achievement is miraculous.

On October 5, 1872, Verlaine informed Blémont that his next collection would contain nothing of his impressions of England. Later he changed his plans. The fourth section of

Romances sans Paroles—"Aquarelles" (Watercolors)—is made
up entirely of English impressions. Exegetists have indulged in
curious speculations about the background of these few poems.
Some have attempted to explain them by experiences Verlaine
had with a number of young Englishwomen. Others have supposed, on the contrary, that behind these figures of women or
girls one should read other kinds of affairs: a gratuitous supposi-
tion that makes proper interpretation of these fine poems more
difficult. It is rather, it would seem, still and always Mathilde
to whom they are addressed. "Green" is the return home, the
reconciliation, the storm and then the calm. "Spleen," the
nostalgia for paradise lost in a heart that is weary of everything,
but not, alas! of Mathilde. And who might that woman who
distresses her poor lover be if not the Mathilde who, for some
time now, has been "dead to [his] heart"?

However sparkling in its own right this poetry is, worthy
researchers have taken it upon themselves to ferret out the
literary texts that may have provided Verlaine with a starting
point, a suggestion. "Green," it has been said, appears to be a
kind of paraphrase of Ophelia's song: "There's rosemary . . . ,
And there are pansies, that's for thoughts . . . , There's fennel
for you, and columbines. There's rue for you. . . ." However,
it has been thought, with perhaps more likelihood, that "Roses
de Saadi," by Marceline Desbordes-Valmore was his source.
"A Poor Young Shepherd," furthermore, was probably sug-
gested to Verlaine by an English text. The February issue of
Gentleman's Magazine, a magazine to which his friend Barrère
contributed, contained a poem on St. Valentine's Day, "A
Valentine," which began with these words: "What should I
send to my beloved? I'll send a kiss to her." A phrase he seems
to pick up and adapt in his first line:

> *J'ai peur d'un baiser.*

> I fear a kiss.

"Child Wife," too, has a literary source. This poem was
written on April 3, 1873, when Verlaine was going to leave
England to take steps in Belgium to effect a reconciliation with
Mathilde. The first draft copy in the British Museum shows
the deletion: "The pretty one." This is a telling particular, for

these words come from an English popular song, "The little pretty one . . ." and Verlaine, at this time, was working, as was Rimbaud, at translating songbooks.

Two of the *aquarelles* were inspired by memories of London. "Streets I" was composed at Hibernia Store, at the corner of Old Compton and Greek Streets. It was there that Vermersch had delivered his lectures. Verlaine saw the jig danced, either in the bar itself, or in the street at the crossing. Like other Frenchmen, he considered the jig a typically English dance, the English dance par excellence.

"Streets II" deals with Regent's Canal, probably at the spot where it comes out of the underground passage that runs under Maida Vale. First it runs straight between Blomfield Road and Maida Hill, banked by two walls. But at Maida Hill it runs along only one wall, just as Verlaine took the trouble to specify in a variant version. The neighborhood is almost rustic, made up of little houses, yellow rather than black cottages, enclosed by gardens. At the point where Regent's Canal joins Grand Junction's Canal, it forms a little lake that surrounds a little green island. One can easily understand why Verlaine should have keenly felt the unexpected picturesque quality of this bit of countryside in the middle of the vast metropolis.

The "Aquarelles" series are last in date of composition among the poems in *Romances sans paroles*. At the time he was writing them, Verlaine had been considering publication of a volume of verse for some time. The notion appears first in a letter dated September 1872. At that date, he had in mind grouping several of the "Paysages belges" into a series that would bear the title "De Charleroi à Londres" (From Charleroi to London). On September 24, the title of the future volume was selected: *Romances sans paroles*. The poet expected the collection to be printed within a month. On October 1, the printing run was imminent. In Verlaine's mind, the whole then formed a series of blurred, sad, and gay impressions, with a touch of the almost simple-mindedly picturesque in "Paysages belges," and an elegiac section that would be a return to *La Bonne Chanson*. But matters dragged on. In December, Verlaine was still hoping that his collection would appear in January. He had divided the poems into four sections: "Romances sans paroles," "Paysages belges," "Nuit falote," and "Birds in the Night." A total of four hundred lines.

A succession of incidents upset these plans. Verlaine considered several publishers, one after the other. In May 1873, he entrusted the manuscript to Lepelletier. The latter reached an agreement with a printer in Sens. Soon thereafter the poet was imprisoned, but he kept up a lively correspondence with his friend. He gave him the most detailed kinds of instructions. In March 1874, *Romances sans paroles* was published, if one may use that word to describe a limited edition of a volume that was not even put on sale. The poems were published in their May 1873 rather than in their December 1872 versions. The first section was now called "Ariettes oubliées." Of the third section, Verlaine had retained but one poem. On the other hand, he had added the English impressions, "Aquarelles," written after December 1872.

6 · The Crowning Work

BEFORE MONS

The manuscript of *Romances sans paroles* had barely been sent off to Lepelletier before Verlaine was contemplating new publications. He was teeming, he said, with new ideas for really fine projects. He considered publishing *Les Vaincus*, of which one section, titled "Sous l'Empire" (Under the Empire), was to include "Le Monstre," "Le Grognard" (The Veteran), "La Soupe du soir," "Crépuscule du matin," and "Les loups," all of which had appeared in magazines from 1867–1869. He said he had a book—perhaps the same—which was to contain a number of sonnets, old pieces from the *saturnien* period, some political verses, and a few obscene poems. Among the latter he placed "Les Amies" (Girl Friends). He dreamed especially of trying out a new poetic form in a volume of *Choses* (Things), which was to include "La Vie au grenier" (Garret Life), "Sous l'Eau" (Underwater), "L'Ile" (The Island), and "Le Sable" (Sand). Each of these poems was to contain from three hundred to four hundred lines. We do not have them, nor do we have the rough drafts or sketches to help us. The references in the *Correspondance* are not such as to give us any definite idea of what they were like. They were about *things*, their goodness, their evil, and man was entirely excluded. They were, Verlaine adds, the pure and unsullied landscapes of a Robinson Crusoe without a Friday. They were both very pictorial and very musical. "L'Ile" was a sumptuous picture of flowers and "La Vie au grenier" a kind of Rembrandt.

Verlaine intended to try a new mode. This consisted, in his mind, of a "system" he hoped to formulate. He dreamed of a reformation, the theory of which he would set forth in the preface of *Les Vaincus*. He proposed therein to do a critique of the poets, of their obvious strainings, their artifices, and their empty eloquence.

Actually the pieces he wrote around this time are very diverse in inspiration, and any attempt to reduce them to a common aesthetic would be a very chancy business. It is possible that Verlaine wrote "La Grâce" (Grace), "Don Juan pipé" (Don Juan Duped), and "L'Impénitence finale" (Final Impenitence) in prison in Brussels; it is more likely, however, that he put the finishing touches on these poems in his cell at the Petits Carmes prison, and that they had been drafted sometime during the preceding months. One editor has supposed that Verlaine wrote them a good many years earlier, that they were youthful works, and that the poet had merely "touched them up." Only a person incapable of reading could come up with such an hypothesis. For the fundamental and central subject of "La Grâce" is a development of the theme of love in the same manner in which Verlaine had just previously expressed it in the fine sonnet, "Invocation," in May 1873; and "Don Juan" takes up the same notion of the sanctity of the flesh that he set forth in the same sonnet.

The truth is that Verlaine was turning back, in a curious way, to a form of antiquated romanticism, which was, one may well believe, far removed from contemporary taste: the fantastic tale, miraculous and religious legend. The author of *Fêtes galantes* and *Romances sans paroles* amuses himself in writing narrative poems of the kind people wrote in Musset's and Gautier's time. He does so with an ease that is extremely ingratiating, with great zest, and sometimes with a touch of bad taste. One hesitates, however, to criticize him for the latter since it is so likely that this bad taste is deliberate and that the poet is encouraging us to laugh a little at ourselves.

The very considerable interest of these poems lies much less in their readability than in the light they shed on certain of Verlaine's and Rimbaud's preoccupations during the last months of their stay in London, just before going to Brussels.

Strange as it may at first seem, the two men dreamed of attaining a state of pure love, in the quietistic sense of the word. A love beyond good and evil, reward and punishment, heaven and hell. A love that is pure in the sense that it is absolute and an end in itself. Equally damned, the two souls in "La Grâce" will find happiness together: the fires of hell and the fires of love intermingle and multiply. It is this new idea of love that prompts Don Juan's revolt. He is the new message. He represents the revolt of the spirit and of the flesh, the emancipation of man and the end of bondage.

It is impossible not to see Rimbaud's influence behind these ideas. The "wholly damned one" in the poem is Rimbaud himself. He is also, in "La Grâce," the assassinated count who asks the countess to go down to hell with him, not to give way, to renounce solitary, banal happiness. Rimbaud, Verlaine said, had all the qualifications needed to be a good Christian: baptism and faith. But he wanted to take the place of God—an enterprise of whose illusory audacity the poet would soon, in Brussels, begin to take the measure. The dissembling Devil jeers at the futile attempt and reminds us that it is not given to man to become Satan.

Closely related to this group of poems in moral intent, but quite different and infinitely superior in artistry and beauty, "Crimen Amoris" was, Verlaine tells us, written in Brussels, in the Petits Carmes, during the very first days of his imprisonment. The allusion in it to the London experience is obvious, and the best commentary on "Crimen Amoris" is Rimbaud's *Saison en enfer* (A Season in Hell). The imagery, however, comes from Baudelaire, and Verlaine's indebtedness to "Les Tentations" (Temptations) in *Petits Poèmes en prose* (Short Prose Poems) has been rightly noted. It is Baudelaire who put the notion of these disturbingly beautiful androgynous demons into his head. His ambition, however, is not to steal a page on the master, but rather to convey, in symbolic guise, Rimbaud's great venture.

Rimbaud, the most beautiful of bad angels. He was sixteen when he came to Paris. He already bore the brand of despair. Nothing but the absolute concerned him. He brought a message —that of the liberation of man through love. Have done with the conflict between good and evil, between the lawful and forbidden, the constant schism that opposes saints and sinners. The balance of two opposing forces is not enough. The best and worst must absorb each into the other, and the seven deadly sins unite with the theological virtues. Only then will universal love reign. This young Satan put a match to the world. That is, he undertook to provide humanity with the model of a liberated life. But when Verlaine wrote "Crimen Amoris," he already knew that the attempt had failed. Failed to the point where not a shred was left behind: a vain dream vanished. And now a new landscape stretches out: a night filled with moonlight on a plain dotted with dark woods and pools. Things in repose worship God. Acceptance has succeeded revolt.

This curious mystery poem is of all Verlaine's poems the one that probably affords the most definite idea of the "system" he was pondering in Jehonville. This luxuriant poetry, full of fires and rubies, this melodious poetry, these subtle meters, the unfolding of these undulating, elusive sentences answer very well to the particulars Verlaine had given his friends around May 1873. In this poem he used an eleven-syllable line, which, he said, was the perfection of incompleteness in that it announced the alexandrine, made it anticipated, then broke off. He makes this line even more flexible by varying the placement of the caesuras from line to line. Thus there is no consistency, no way to anticipate the meter and find in the fulfillment of that anticipation an easy satisfaction. As one fine Belgian critic, Marcel Thiry, has said, Verlaine makes the *poem* disappear in order that the *poetry*, in its purest state, may shine forth.

At this same period, early in his prison term, Verlaine composed a number of other pieces. These were later to be collected in *Parallèlement* (Parallelly). One of these, then titled "Promenade au préau" (Walk in the Prisonyard), yields a most valuable bit of information. When he sent it to Lepelletier, Verlaine prefaced it with the following remark: "This is the old system: too easy to do and much less amusing to read, isn't it?" Let us apply the fact to the poet. With this mastery of expression, this detachment that allows him to take up at will one or another key signature, he amuses himself by writing at the very same time according to two different "systems"; and when we compare "Promenade au préau" to "Crimen Amoris," for example, or to "Invocation" (later the sonnet "Luxures"—Lust), we can finally understand the true significance of the poetic discoveries that Verlaine imparted to his friends from Jehonville in the spring of 1873. For "Promenade au préau" is a delightful work. It would be far from out of place following *Romances sans paroles*. It is rich in subtle and graphic details. Its meter evokes the tread of the prisoners, the sound of their boots on the flagstones of the yard. It is a fine example of Impressionist poetry. Actually, however, Verlaine has broken with impressionism.

Having exhausted its potential, he is now discovering its limits. A poet has better things to do than merely record impressions. He must penetrate beyond, into the mysterious core of things, he must, by way of appearances, pierce through to reality, which is spirit. Deeper than mere sensation, the poet must apprehend, within himself, the tragedy of man, pierce as far as those retreats where the soul chooses between good and evil, between acceptance and revolt; he must paint the heartbreaks, hopes for freedom, and the failures that comprise the pathos of our fate. It is the poet's task to define and discover the mysterious correspondence between the secret life of the soul and that of things. The sensible world is no longer for Verlaine a pretext for graphic notations. It becomes the mirror of his fate, the reflection of his disasters and his hopes. In Verlaine's work, true symbolism, no longer the amusing play of synaesthetic experience but rather the poetry of the invisible and the beyond, is born in 1873.

Again one feels the influence of Rimbaud behind these ideas. Delahaye, his most intimate confidant, emphasized his desire to return to poetry the significance it had lost. He saw art, said Delahaye, only as a means of exposing the masses to the idea of revolt through brotherhood and love. He had nothing but scorn for men of letters and aesthetes. Aesthetes meaning, of course, Parnassians of the Mendès genre. But aesthetes also in the sense of collectors of *impressions* in the manner of Mérat. Poetry was a more serious affair; it was a sacred work, the fulfillment of a mission, revelation. From these ideas of Rimbaud, Verlaine culled all that a man and poet of his temperament could cull.

Rimbaud, furthermore, introduced him to the works of a number of writers to whom he had not previously paid much attention. We know this for certain in the case of Marceline Desbordes-Valmore. It was Rimbaud who "forced" Verlaine to read all of the poetess' works at a time when he considered them no more than "a hotchpotch with a few spots of beauty." We may believe that it was Rimbaud again who opened his eyes to the real value of the Romantic school. We know the scorn the Parnassians showed for Lamartine and Musset. These are the two poets Verlaine now esteems most. Not, we suspect, the Lamartine of *Les Méditations*, but the too little read poet of *La Chute d'un ange* (The Fall of an Angel). By the spring of 1873, Verlaine entertains a lasting admiration for him. Later he will place him next to Baudelaire. In naming the greatest poets of French literature he will from that time on cite Lamartine and Musset. At no time will he name Victor Hugo. In Marceline Desbordes-Valmore's work, he liked the unceasing flow of images, the spontaneous outbursts which bespoke a lofty and sensitive soul. He noted with particular attention her use of the eleven-syllable line. And it is from her that he took over the couplet, that so little practiced yet so moving form which corresponds more than any other, in French verse, to the verses of the Book of Psalms in the Bible.

IN THE MONS PRISON

One might suppose that Verlaine would spend his first few months in prison without writing anything. However, he had been transferred to Mons for hardly more than a few weeks when he was contemplating a new volume and was composing one of his best works—the admirable series that comprises "Mon Almanach pour 1874" (My Calendar for 1874). At this time his poetry begins to reflect his own internal drama, his depressions, his strivings toward a cleansed and happy life. And from this time on the religious impulse engages him, and he writes "Cantiques à Marie" (Canticles to Mary) and "Prières de la primitive église" (Prayers of the Early Christian Church).

However, another hypothesis must be given. On leaving prison, Verlaine put together a manuscript in which he assembled poems presumably written in Brussels and Mons between July 1873 and January 1875. He gave it the title *Cellulairement* (Cellularly). This precious notebook was seen and studied by Ernest Dupuy, and that fine critic came to the conclusion that he had in hand the first drafts of the poems Verlaine wrote in prison. He further concluded that every confidence was to be accorded to the manuscript indications as to the date and circumstances of the composition of these poems without reservation. V. P. Underwood, however, has satisfactorily demonstrated that this notebook was made up in Stickney; and that Verlaine arranged the poems in the collection not in actual order of composition but, for purposes of symmetry, according to a preconceived plan; and that he dated them with the settings where the poems take place in mind. The consequences of this demonstration are important. The only poems we have that were certainly written in prison are those that Verlaine sent to Lepelletier during his eighteen months at Mons, that is, "Almanach pour 1874," the sonnet sequence "Jésus m'a dit . . ." (Jesus Told Me . . .), and a few short pieces. As for the others, a doubt that cannot for the moment be dispelled remains.

One has the impression from these poems that Verlaine is making his way in the direction he set for himself in the spring of 1873. Although "Promenade au préau" is written according to "the old system," and "Pouacre" (Vermin) gives the impression of being an "old *poème saturnien*," the "Almanach" and the sonnets in the "Jésus m'a dit . . ." sequence continue the admirable advance in his work at this time. The most beautiful and the most characteristic piece in the "Almanach"—"Eté" (Summer)—is pure symbol. Not description and impression, but transposition. The overwhelming heat, the ice-water thirst, the obsessive buzzing of the wasp, the dark room crossed by rays of light exist only as symbols of a crushed soul, plunged into a darkness pierced by a few glimmerings of hope. Similarly symbolic are the sonnets Verlaine composed the day after August 15, 1874, that is—if his own calculations are accurate—on the day after he made confession and took Communion. Their admirable strength and their overwhelming humility have been quite rightly singled out for praise. Equally worthy of attention, however, from a purely poetic point of view, is the boldness of the use of metaphor, which embodies spiritual truths in terms of artistic beauty. When Verlaine writes:

> O *Ma nuit claire! ô tes yeux dans Mon clair de lune!*
> *O ce lit de lumière et d'eau parmi la brume!*
> *Toute cette innocence et tout ce reposoir!*

> O My bright night! O your eyes by My bright moon!
> O this bed of light and water 'mid the gloom!
> All this innocence, this holy resting-place!

he is not only a great religious poet, but an artist, a creator of pure beauty.

If one is to trust the double evidence of the manuscript of *Cellulairement* and a letter to Valade, it was in Mons, in April 1874, that Verlaine wrote one of his best-known works, "Art poétique" (The Art of Poetry). This delightful work has perhaps suffered from a superfluity of explication. The text itself presents no mystery. But exegetists have so inflated it with intentions, have so exaggerated its import that it is necessary to linger a bit over these few stanzas and determine their exact significance. Verlaine said: "Don't take my 'Art poétique' literally—it is only a song"; and this warning should be respected by all who undertake its explication.

We now know that it was not in April 1874, that Verlaine's poetry took a new turn. We know that he had long since broken with Parnasse and that consequently he would not have considered announcing this break in April 1874. We also know that from the spring of 1873 on he had moved away from impressionism and that even his *Romances sans paroles* no longer represents his poetic preferences. His "Art poétique" is not a canon, and Verlaine is not interested in laying down laws. It is as pure poet that he speaks. He describes what poetry is to him—a kind of music, a quiver of the soul, a flight to other climes and loves. He speaks of liberation from old constraints; and it is not his fault if he finds in his path the most constraining of poetics, that of Parnasse, with its exigencies of rhyme, its taste for brilliant colors and oversharp contours. Stifling technique, but above all a technique that obstructs the poet's flight, that deceives, that finds poetry in precisely that which is its opposite. In "Art poétique" Verlaine reminded his contemporaries, as he reminds all of us, of the true significance of poetry, its purely spiritual value.

SAGESSE

It was not in Mons but after he left prison—in Stickney—that Verlaine once again felt his confidence and energy revive. His activities at the time were divided among several projects. First he considered renewing ties with the Paris literary world, with those Parnassians from whom he felt removed, but who were, nevertheless, in 1875, the only group by whom he could get his poems accepted. He had learned that a third *Parnasse* collection was being prepared. Around July 1, 1875, he sent a contribution to Emile Blémont. He waited several months for an answer. In September, he learned that the *Komité des grâces* (Dispensation Kommittee), as he called it, was firmly against him. Leconte de Lisle, Banville, Coppée, and Anatole France were responsible for making the decisions. These men could manage to overcome neither their political grudges nor the straitness of their taste. In October they rejected the exile's poems. A stupid decision, but one that today does Verlaine honor; he had been rejected together with Mallarmé. *L'Après-midi d'un faune* (The Afternoon of a Faun) had been no more favored than Verlaine's verses by the augurers.

During this same period he was preparing *Cellulairement* for publication. From Stickney he sent the contents of this volume, a hundred lines at a time, to Delahaye in France. Starting around the end of May 1875, these dispatches went on until October 26, 1875. At that date *Cellulairement* contained thirty-two poems and eighteen hundred lines altogether. In it were to be found the series from "Mon Almanach pour 1874," the diabolical tales, "Crimen Amoris," "Art poétique," a few very beautiful poems inspired by his prison experience, the series "Vieux Coppées" (Old Coppées), and, to finish up, the ten sonnets of "Jésus m'a dit. . . ." Verlaine hoped the collection would be printed at Charleville. The enterprise fell through, and Verlaine quickly turned his attention to another undertaking. In a letter of November 19, 1875, he no longer says a word about *Cellulairement* and announces that he has two volumes in the works—*Sagesse* (Wisdom) and *Amour* (Love).

Since leaving prison his ambition had been to hymn his new convictions in a great religious work. In April 1875, he was working on a group of spiritual canticles. He projected a huge poem to be titled "Le Rosaire" (The Rosary). This was to be immense, embracing all civilizations and all legends. In the center, the figure of the Virgin. Verlaine envisaged four to five thousand lines. Having become a legitimist, he also considered writing a patriotic book. With no further delay, he undertook the composition of two books in which he would express his convictions, his courage, and his happiness. The poems he then composed he divided, somewhat indiscriminately, between *Sagesse* and *Amour*.

Indeed, he did not confine himself to gathering up old pieces or dreaming of vague projects. He wrote, and the poems born of his inspiration at this time are probably the most beautiful of all his works. If it is possible, in this poet's life, to discern and affirm the existence of a high point, in an output so abundant and rich in masterpieces to discover a peak, the Stickney, Boston, and Bournemouth years are clearly that high point and mark that peak. It was in July and August 1875, that he wrote the overwhelming poem:

> *O mon Dieu, vous m'avez blessé d'amour* . . .

> O my Lord, you have wounded me with love . . .

and

> *Je ne veux plus aimer que ma mère Marie,*

> Henceforth I wish to love none but my mother Mary,

worthy sequels to "Jésus m'a dit. . . ." They have the same mystique of personal union with Christ, the same feeling of trusting humility, the same highly skillful execution in what appears to be a natural and spontaneous outpouring.

It was doubtless a bit later, in 1876 and the beginning of 1877 —when the humble life and discipline were beginning to pall on him—that he wrote three splendid sonnets that may be ranked among his greatest masterpieces: "O vous comme un qui boite au loin . . ." (O you, like someone limping in the distance . . .),

"Les faux beaux jours ont lui . . ." (The false, the lovely days have shone . . .) and, to a lesser degree, "La vie humble aux travaux ennuyeux et faciles . . ." (The humble life of tiresome and easy duties . . .). The breadth of stroke, the strength of line, the bold freedom of style are witness, in Verlaine's poetry, to the persistence of the goals he set in 1873 and to their admirable fruition. Almost no more sentences, or verbs: successive flashes of light, abruptly introduced metaphors. No gratuitous picturesqueness, no detail for its mere pleasantness, rather, the most sparing, the most austere of arts. Sometimes an image flashes, not a stock figure but an image taken from everyday reality:

> *Vieux bonheurs, vieux malheurs, comme une file d'oies*
> *Sur la route en poussière où tous les pieds ont lui,*
> *Bon voyage!*

> Old fortunes, old misfortunes, like a queue of geese
> On the dusty track whereon all feet have shone,
> Bon voyage!

Finally, in these poems appears, in all its splendor, that genuine symbolism which was the great discovery of 1873, that advance over impressionism and its too facile charms. Let us look closely at "Les faux beaux jours ont lui . . . ." There is no question here of impressions gathered on a stormy evening. The subject of these lines is a sinner's soul, returned to virtue, which feels old temptations rumbling. This agitation, this anguish, this flight toward the Lord of Mercy are not directly expressed by the poet as formerly the joys and purities of *La Bonne Chanson* were. His whole poem is one single metaphor. A stormy landscape, a lurid light, the slopes of the valley lashed by the downpour. But in the distance another prospect—one of clear skies, of silence, and of prayer. A woman passes, eyes lowered, hands clasped: the soul of the poet as it must become and must remain.

Side by side with these pieces that continue and crown previous effort, that are allied with and extend that effort, are others that put us in the presence of an unexpected poetic world. In these, allegories come to life. Here the brave knight Misfortune plunges his iron fingers into the poet's breast and causes a new heart to be born therein. And here a lady in snow-white raiment descends from the sky and puts the monster, the fierce giant, Flesh, to flight. This lady is Prayer. And here the allegory of a besieged city, maintained despite betrayals from within, betrayals that would hand over the keys of the city to the usurping enemy. These works show a new impulse in Verlaine's work. One is tempted to suppose that he had become acquainted, in some unknown manner, with old French allegorical literature. It is much more likely, however, that it was through English poetry, in Bunyan and in the more recent works of Tennyson, that Verlaine became acquainted with this kind of poetry, which is one of the traditional genres of English literature.

V. P. Underwood's diligent researches have established the overall similarity of impulse among certain English allegorical works and these poems in *Sagesse*. However, these researches have not succeeded in uncovering specific cases of imitation or any direct relationship. Nor have they succeeded in proving that the religious poems in *Sagesse* were directly inspired by the *Book of Hymns* of the Anglican Church. They have, in any case, however, brought to light strong and numerous similarities. Verlaine admired the spare beauty of the *Hymns*, in which Biblical poetry mingled with ancient Christian liturgy and in which the old faith had for centuries been expressed in the most moving of forms. Perhaps he wished to give back to the French people a form of poetry from which they had, since the time of Marot and Goudimel, been little by little cut off. Cazals, in any case, wrote in 1896: "It was in England that he produced that transcendant work, *Sagesse,* inspired," he affirmed, "by those English songs he never tired of listening to and that he never heard without being indescribably affected." Such pieces as:

> *Va ton chemin sans plus t'inquiéter* . . .
>
> Go your way no longer troubled . . .

and

> *Pourquoi triste, ô mon âme,*
> *Triste jusqu'à la mort* . . .
>
> Why sorrowful, oh my soul,
> Sorrowful unto death . . .

are probably examples of lines inspired by songs of the Anglican liturgy.

If we had, analogous to Underwood's, a study of the Catholic sources of the poetry of *Sagesse*, we might be able more accurately to define the stages of religious inspiration between Verlaine's conversion and the publication of that collection. He had, from the time of his months in prison, the worthy ambition of making his faith the very lifeblood of his intellect and, consequently, of nourishing that intellect by extensive reading. He kept to this program during his stay in England. In April 1875, he became aware of his "metaphysical eyes," and he wrote to Delahaye that he was in the midst of "plunging into all the problems." In September we find him buried in Aquinas, and he had just bought the works of Saint Teresa. In Rethel he made further progress; there one finds him steeping himself in works of ascetic theology.

The research has not been done, or has not been done with the necessary systematic effort and patience. It would, however, be interesting to know by what means Verlaine became acquainted with those stirring texts of Saint Bonaventure and Saint Catherine of Siena which he used at this time as epigraphs to his poems, and especially to know if he knew more of these masters of spiritual life than a few phrases picked up in the course of his studies. The problem, which is one of the most difficult, has been considerably clarified by the discovery of a notebook in which Verlaine made notes on his reading and scribbled a few thoughts during his Mons and Stickney years.

Of the works of religion that the new convert owns or has at his disposal for study, the Bible and the Breviary turn up often, and one divines, from the passages he quotes, that he approached them as poet as well as believer. He also owns copies of Saint Jeanne de Chantal and of Bossuet's *Méditations*. He notes—probably because he intends to read them—"Mystiques espagnols [Spanish Mystics]: Louis de Grenade, Louis de León, Jean d'Avila, sainte Thérèse." But he also owns several copies of Aquinas' *Summa Theologica* and several volumes by Joseph de Maistre and Balmès. He seems to have attached particular interest to Auguste Nicolas' *Etudes philosophiques sur le christianisme* (Philosophical Studies in Christianity). He retains in his movings about several apologetical treatises. We find this Christian, whom one might have supposed wholly instinctive, constantly concerned with justifying and confirming his faith through knowledge.

A worthy preoccupation that does him honor. It sheds light, however, on the unmistakable falling-off in his poems of 1877–1880. One observes in his work for the first time errors in taste, lapses. Certain stanzas, for instance, on Paris, which were probably written around September 1877, are not lacking in beauty, but they end badly, in bombast and redundancy:

> De près, de loin, le Sage aura sa thébaïde
> Parmi le fade ennui qui tombe de ceci
> D'autant plus âpre et plus sanctifiante aussi
> Que deux parts de son âme y pleurent, dans ce vide!

> From near or far the Sage shall have his Thebaid
> From out the dull ennui that comes from this,
> The harsher, the more sanctifying too
> The more his soul's two parts weep on it in this void!

The poems that follow, in *Sagesse*, are in the same style. The description of Arras has the prosaic quality of a piece by Coppée. "Fête du blé" (Wheat Festival) is better; but examined closely, its eloquence seems a bit empty, and it has a romantic wordiness that brings to mind a lesser Lamartine.

The fact is that during these years Verlaine is less interested in creating works of poetry than in expressing in verse his intellectual preoccupations and the dogmatism of the recent convert. He is convinced that art is human vanity. Since he goes on writing verses, a goodly number of verses, does he still believe in poetry? In sending Charles de Sivry, for Mathilde's attention, the exquisite poem:

> Ecoutez la chanson bien douce
> Qui ne pleure que pour vous plaire . . .

> Listen to the gentle song
> That only weeps to please you . . .

he attached the shocking remark: "I should title it Pickity-Peckity, Goody-Goody, and it strikes me, as any Parisese effort, as stupid, utterly stupid! Well, anyway, here's this pretty little

tune, which shows no talent, I fear." We are thus, alas! fore-
warned. When Verlaine, in Rethel, touched once more on the
pure inspiration of former times, he was the first to laugh:
Parisese effort, mere tunemaking.

Because he has put his talent in the service of an orthodoxy,
the poems of this period are written in an abstract language in
which the coldest kinds of entities clash, in sentences that are
both halting and complex. By way of example, consider these
dreary lines:

> *Colères, soupirs noirs, regrets, tentations,*
> *Qu'il a fallu pourtant que nous entendissions*
> *Pour l'assourdissement des silences hônnetes,*
> *Colères, soupirs noirs, regrets, tentations . . .*

> Cholers, dark sighings, regrets, and temptations,
> To which, nonetheless, we had to lend attention
> In order to muffle the unoccupied silences,
> Cholers, dark sighings, regrets, and temptations . . .

At this time Verlaine composed his celebrated sonnet:

> *Non. Il fut gallican, ce siècle, et janséniste!*
> *C'est vers le Moyen âge énorme et délicat*
> *Qu'il faudrait que mon coeur en panne naviguât*
> *Loin de nos jours d'esprit charnel et de chair triste.*

> No, Gallican this century, and Jansenist!
> It's to the vast and purer Middle Ages
> My hove-to heart must navigate
> Far from these times of carnal mind, of woeful flesh.

To the Middle Ages, indeed. But not to the Middle Ages of
tender poems of courtly love; nor to that of realistic and ironical
tales and farces. But rather to the Middle Ages of the *Summa
Theologica* and didactic poems, to the least ingenuous and most
intensely rationalist of Middle Ages, the one against which
Thomas à Kempis' *De Imitatione Christi* was written. The
Rethel poems, indeed, recall that Middle Ages—in their abstract-
ness and in their awkwardness.

Verlaine's Catholicism bore, from the first, the stamp of
Joseph de Maistre. It had been marked as well by Barbey

d'Aurevilly, and it is no surprise to learn that the poet had his *Prophètes du Passé* (Prophets of the Past) in his own library. He also owned a three-volume *Histoire des Jésuites* (History of the Jesuits) and a life of Marguerite-Marie Alacoque. These help to explain his loathing of democracy and the Republican regime. The jottings of Delahaye, and of Verlaine and Germain Nouveau, prove to what extent, around 1880, these neophytes confused religion and politics. And this throws light on the patriotic and legitimist poems in *Sagesse*. Alas! Verlaine does not have the great allure of Barbey d'Aurevilly. One feels him more narrowminded, more nagging. His poems lack both verve and taste.

Sagesse had been in preparation since 1875 and was still not finished. One should recall the events that marked these years in Verlaine's life. In 1877, the return to France and the teaching job in Rethel. In August 1879, the fresh departure for England, the months in Lymington and, at the end of December, the definitive return to France. In March 1880, the purchase of the farm in Juniville. During these years of solitude, far from Paris, without contact, even by mail, with his old friends, out of touch with publishers, Verlaine time and again delayed printing his book. Finally, in 1880, he got in touch with the Société Générale de Librairie Catholique (General Society of Catholic Publishing). Once again he was obliged to pay publication costs. The edition was set for five hundred copies and cost him five hundred and forty-seven and a half francs. The volume came out around the beginning of December 1880, with the date 1881 on the cover. It received a considerable amount of publicity, but not enough to break the conspiracy of silence that had grown up around the prisoner of Mons. In his naïveté Verlaine thought that the Catholic audience would take him up and provide the means of revenging the disdain of the men of letters. *Sagesse* did not sell. It is said that the publisher, overcrowded by this useless stock of books, had them stored in the cellar.

It is important that anyone wishing to do justice to this masterpiece of French poetry should first divest himself of one long-standing error. Talking about *Sagesse* as if Verlaine, at the period of publication, had stopped believing and worshipping is out of the question. It is shocking that people have imagined him smiling hypocritically when, in the last months of 1880, he corrected the proofs of his book. The long-standing misconception about the real nature of his friendship for Lucien Létinois explains why people have not recognized the truth— that *Sagesse* is the sincerest kind of statement, an impassioned declaration of faith, the confession of a man who put himself wholly into his work. Sincerity is not a literary virtue, and it is not because of its genuineness that *Sagesse* is an admirable book. But since there are some historians who would claim that these outpourings are mendacious, it is necessary to set the facts straight and to assert that Verlaine wrote this book with his whole soul.

On the other hand, it is absurd to praise *Sagesse* as a "highly coherent" work, for the sole fault one may truly attribute to this volume is that of being a composite work, of mixing together poems of quite obviously different date, impulse, and quality. In making it up, Verlaine dismembered *Cellulairement*, shifted seven pieces of this 1875 manuscript to the 1880 book. Then he added the poems written in England, most of them very good ones, but also the inferior ones from the Rethel period, and some of very recent composition. This ensemble, made up of poems spread out over a period of nearly seven years, presents disparities that strike the eye of even the least informed reader.

But this same ensemble has as well a richness, variety, and more often than not a beauty that make *Sagesse* Verlaine's masterwork. We are perhaps ill prepared for understanding what was original and valuable about this book. We are not sufficiently aware of the degree to which French poetry during the previous fifteen years had tended to restrict itself to the description of appearances. Whether it gave itself over to the empty mannerisms of exoticism or, contrarily, concentrated on recording the familiar picturesque quality of everyday life, poetry, in the work of many, had hardly any aim but that of seeing and describing. Sometimes an effort was made to convey modern anxieties and despairs; but again, this effort did not go beyond the level of appearances. The mysterious reality of the soul, the backgrounds, the perspectives, were lost to this poetry.

7 · Last Works

THE LAST YEARS

It was from Juniville that Verlaine had supervised the publication of *Sagesse*. He was still the man one no longer knew. It was not until 1882, after the liquidation of his farm enterprise, when he had nothing left but to try his chances in Paris, that he got in touch once more with the literary circles of the capital. He depended for this on Lepelletier's friendship. The latter introduced him to the editors of *Réveil* (Awakening). He introduced him to his newspaper colleagues, who held their meetings at the Brasserie Bergère. Verlaine could be seen at the cafés D'Harcourt, La Source, and the Louis XIII. He was often alone. Sometimes Germain Nouveau was with him. The new groups were wholly unacquainted with his work. Only Valade and Mérat still remembered him, and Raoul Ponchon is said, on one occasion, to have quoted a couplet from one of his old poems. At the time the poet Rollinat reigned in Montmartre.

Verlaine, however, was still full of courage and, as he wrote to one correspondent, he was "absolutely resolved to take up the fight again, in prose and in verse, and in the theatre and in journalism when necessary." In July 1882, he succeeded in placing several poems in *Paris-Moderne*, a magazine published by Vanier that printed the verses of Leconte de Lisle, Banville, and Mendès, but of others as well—Mérat and Valade, for instance. Then in November, Verlaine sent, among other poems, his "Art poétique" to the same magazine. This poem made a stir in avant-

garde circles. The *Nouvelle Rive Gauche* (New Left Bank),
which had just that month begun to appear, devoted an article
to him. It was signed Karl Mohr. This was Charles Morice, a
young man of twenty-one. His article was severe. It criticized
Verlaine as being a dangerous model for young writers. But it
was attentive. Verlaine wrote to Charles Morice, and almost
immediately became a regular contributor to the review. When,
in April 1883, it changed format and took the title of *Lutèce*
(Lutetia), he continued to remain associated with it. Rodolphe
Salis's *Chat Noir* (Black Cat) welcomed him in turn. From
May 1883 on, Verlaine wrote for *the* magazine of Montmartre.

He established firm friendships: with Charles Morice, and
at the beginning of 1883 with Moréas. He met him at the
D'Harcourt, the Voltaire, in the offices of *Chat Noir*. This was
the period when Verlaine and his mother were living in the
modest but reasonably comfortable apartment on Rue de la
Roquette. Madame Verlaine cheerfully received her son's new
friends there. Moréas and Morice were to be seen in her living
room, as well as Léo Trézenik, Valadon, and Ernest Raynaud.

Shortly thereafter Verlaine left Paris. This was the start of
the dismal Coulommes period. But he did not allow himself
to be forgotten. Beginning with the August 24, 1883, issue,
Lutèce printed his *Poètes maudits* (Condemned Poets): first,
Tristan Corbière, then Rimbaud, then Mallarmé. This time
success came. Although these studies may seem to us rather
hastily put together and superficially grounded, they struck the
young people of 1883 as a manifesto. They introduced them to
the true values of their times. The following year the message
reached the general public—through Huysmans, who, in *A
Rebours* (Against the Grain), introduced the author of *Sagesse*.
In three pages of excellent criticism, he praised the originality
of Verlaine's poetry; he subtly analysed and revealed in felicitous
phrases what was extraordinary about this poetry of "shadowy
and delightful disclosures" made "in an undertone at twilight,"
about the "disturbing reaches of the soul," the "so muted
whisperings of thoughts" to be found in this work. The best
minds were reached: Laforgue read and liked several of the
melancholy sonnets; on May 24, 1883, he wrote in his notebook:

"Verlaine, what a real poet! He is indeed the one to whom I am closest."

In 1885, when Verlaine returned to Paris, he took stock of his increasing fame. He abandoned his intention of throwing himself into the fray. On October 1, he wrote Vanier: "Zut, I'm burning my ships. Fanfare and fife!" Others are now added to his 1883 acquaintances. In 1886, we see Jules Tellier, François-Maurice du Plessys, and Rachilde around with him. He also becomes friendly with Edouard Dujardin and with René Ghil, who had sent him his *Légende d'âmes et de sang* (Legend of Souls and of Blood). He emerges now as a kind of literary leader.

Two schools were taking shape within the young poetic movement. The first of these inclined to a very intellectual kind of poetry, a poetry charged with hidden meanings supported by high metaphysical intent. It claimed Wagner and Mallarmé as masters. People were beginning to apply the term "Symbolists" to this group. The others, who lived mainly in the Montagne Sainte-Geneviève area, remained faithful to "the Left Bank spirit" and called for a more direct, more open poetry, one more concerned with expressing modern sensibility and aspirations. The name "Décadents" was applied to them. They claimed Verlaine as their master.

A close look at the swarm of little magazines in 1885–1886 makes it clear that the division is fairly sharp. It is true that Verlaine contributed indiscriminately to any and all who would take his poems or his prose work and pay for them. But he was really at home only in *Lutèce*, and that magazine was, on the whole, hostile to the Symbolist faction. It was in sympathy with *Le Scapin* and *Le Décadent*, which also had the Left Bank spirit. And it did not share in the high pretensions of *La Vogue* and *Revue wagnérienne*.

Verlaine pretended not to know what this title of leader of a school which the young were agreed in bestowing on him was all about. In October 1885, he alluded to it: "He is quite aware," he wrote, "that people attribute a school to him. A school to Verlaine! A school that would itself declare itself Decadent." In reality he took the role that had fallen to him very seriously, and the best proof of this is doubtless the establishment of the "Wednesdays" he was to initiate as soon as circumstances permitted. He was aware of being the source and remaining at the center of a new poetic movement. He defined this movement precisely when, in his biography of Baju, he recalled the origins of the *Ecole décadente*: "a certain number of young people, weary of forever reading the same dismal, so-called naturalist horrors, belonging moreover to a more disillusioned generation than any previous, but for that all the more anxious to have a literature that reflected its yearnings toward a profound and serious ideal, and somewhat indifferent to Parnassian serenity, one day took it into their heads to read my poems." Reaction against Naturalism and against Parnasse, an idealistic poetry, expressing both anxiety and high aspirations: the whole meaning of Decadence, in the sense that Verlaine attributed to the word, is summed up here.

One can see how far this Decadence—in the sense Verlaine insisted on—was from "fin de siècle" pessimism and morbidity. The notion of Decadence had appeared in 1881 in a study by Bourget on Baudelaire. It was embodied in 1884 in the character of Des Esseintes in Huysmans' *A Rebours*. Newspapermen and critics fancied that the Decadent was nourished by Schopenhauer and Hartmann, and they found in Darwin the reasons for giving way to despair. Verlaine, on the contrary, wanted the young school to react against this pessimism, against the clichés of a literature of despondency, and to be healthy and discerning. Verlaine's statements on contemporary poetry are clarified by a thought which he himself did not express but which one perceives to be understood: and that is that the new school already has its masterwork, its model, the book that expresses its ideals in sovereign fashion, and that that book is *Sagesse*. *Decadence*, in Verlaine's mind, is quite the opposite of *deterioration*, with which a number of people confused it.

Understood thus, Decadence discloses its true sources, its first masters. These are two men who, in a period when materialism was triumphant, maintained—alone, and gamely—the cause of idealism: Barbey d'Aurevilly and Villiers de l'Ile-Adam. Verlaine had admired the first since 1873 and had been a friend of the second for a long time. It is with them he joins, it is their flag he raises, and their enemies will from this time on be his enemies.

Formed by Verlaine, the young school reacted first and foremost against naturalist materialism. It asserted the realities of the soul. It would not accept the view that man is the mere product and result of a particular set of circumstances and biological makeup. It was equally opposed to the Parnassian tradition, to the concept of an art that chills and isolates him from life. The watchword of these young Decadents, liegemen of Verlaine, and successors to Barbey, is *Life*. Life intense, life rich and subtle, the life of the soul torn between the dual injunctions of lust and of the ideal, between Satan and God. Poetry should grasp the "rare, intimate, hidden" aspects of life.

In the area of expression, the Decadents enlarged upon and systematized Verlaine's "Art poétique." No magniloquence in the Romantic, or more specifically, the Victor Hugo manner. No description. Give the sensation of things, the impression of objects. Because only the *self* is important. The external world merely furnishes the poet sensations which he cultivates in reverie in order to grasp their most delicate nuances. The style should be uncommon and abrupt, the stroke rapid and connotative, in order to record the idea in all its complexity and make it loom up in all its power.

This doctrine of Decadence corresponds too precisely to Verlaine's work not to be also the echo of his teaching. Despite the pedantic cast it took in the magazines (this whole decade is given to pedanticism), the Decadent aesthetic expressed an effort toward a flavorful simplicity, a subtle clarity, and a rejection of systems and metaphysics. It was thereby opposed to the Symbolists and tended to set Verlaine up against Mallarmé. In certain respects, however, their works converged. Both expected evocation of poetry, an invitation to construct and dream. Both condemned that absurd kind of realism that claims to make, with words, a copy of objects, a kind of exact and total reproduction of the real. It is nonetheless true that Verlaine, in private, and his friends, in public, expressed no liking for the Mallarmean school. Beginning in 1885, Verlaine's magazine, *Lutèce*, writing in reference to Laforgue's *Complaintes*, accused "les Mallarmé" of having "fraudulently thrown art into a rut," and Léo Trézenik did not conceal the fact that he considered Mallarmé responsible for Laforgue's failure, for the impenetrability of his indecipherable *Complaintes*, for the "ink-pot" school he chose to preside over. One of Verlaine's letters, written in October 1887, speaks in lively fashion of Mallarmé's "foolishnesses."

How can some historians claim that these quarrels and op-positions were of no account when actually they put the very essence of poetry into question? And, as regards Verlaine, how not see that it was his influence that hung in the balance? For the choice to be made, for the young poets, was between the metaphysical poetry that looked to Mallarmé for authority, and that "poetry of life" that recognized Verlaine as true master. Little by little, certain of his disciples fell away. By 1886, Moréas and René Ghil are no longer Verlaine supporters. Vielé-Griffin and Henri de Régnier, won over momentarily, pass over to the Symbolist camp. In October Ghil announces his break. He declares a "total split with the so-called students of Verlaine." Guy Michaud, in his "Message du symbolisme," fixes January 1887, as the date when the whole group of Ghil, Stuart Merrill, Vielé-Griffin, and Régnier became conscious of the conflict between Mallarmé and Verlaine and without hesi-tation opted for the master of the Rue de Rome.

One cannot reproach Verlaine for having exasperated his antagonists. Rather, it is surprising how long it took him to become aware of them—unless one keeps in mind the circum-stances of his life in 1886 and 1887. For a long time he fol-lowed the controversies of the Symbolists and Decadents with disdainful amusement. On November 22, 1886, he wrote to Jules Tellier: "The quarrel between the Symbolists, Decadents, and other euphuists has died down." A month later, in the most disinterested tone: "All the scribblings of the Decadent thing have dropped out of sight." At this date, the word "Decadent" seemed absurd to him: "What a stupid word!" he wrote to Lepelletier; and on February 15, 1887, in a letter to Coppée, he poked fun at "our symbolants and other decadists." Simi-larly, in June, he again made fun of "all these symbolo and decadard ephebes." The only disciples he recognized at that date were Baju, Du Plessys, and Ernest Raynaud. He was already forming in his mind the idea that there is no theory capable of containing the fact of poetry, that all poetics are equally futile, and that the poet's only function is to sing. In August 1887, Vielé-Griffin asked him for a statement of principles. He replied tartly: "Everything is beautiful and good that is beautiful and good, no matter where it comes from or by what means it is obtained. Classicists, Romantics, Decadents, Symbolists, Assonantists or, what should I call them, deliberate obscurantists, so long as they give me a chill or just charm me, are all fine with me."

Thus he would never have openly taken sides if certain provocations had not forced him to do so. The month of September 1887 can be set as the beginning of this change in attitude. "We are being challenged," he wrote to Vanier. In November he expressed his readiness to intervene. He noted that the public was ill-informed about him. At the same time that some were criticizing him for having "fallen into the pagoda of Monsieur Mallarmé," others chose to set him up against the author of *L'Après-midi d'un faune*. He felt the need to clear the air, to state his position clearly, with no nonsense and no backtracking.

Thus he took sides, and that openly, with the Decadents, while Mallarmé became the leading figure of the Symbolists. On November 25, 1887, he discussed several projects for *Le Décadent* with Baju. In December he gave this magazine a "Ballade pour les décadents" (Ballad for the Decadents). His biography of Baju in *Hommes d'aujourd'hui* (Men of Today) was a very clear statement of principles.

Then in a very short time—January 1888—there was at least a parting of the ways if not a quarrel. *Le Décadent* had, against his express wishes, published his "Ballade touchant un point d'histoire" (Ballad Touching on a Point of History). He was not kept informed of the activities of the group to which he had lent his name. Therefore he withdrew. Here are the terms in which he announced his intentions to Dr. Jullien: "I am having trouble with the Decadents. I have a good mind to leave that clearly compromising nursery in peace. How dumb and hateful people are, even the best of them. . . ." Actually, he continued to give *Le Décadent* a few poems up to July. But none after that.

Verlaine had shown uncommon discretion about one of the most often discussed subjects in the recent controversies—rhyme. His "Art poétique," to which young writers had been exposed in 1882, did not aim at doing away with rhyme but only reacted against using it to excess. When certain collections in which traditional prosody was openly defied came out, he called on these audacious authors to exercise caution. In a letter to Gustave Kahn in August 1887, he congratulated the poet on his daring, on his "delectable subtleties," and on his "felicitous ellipses." But he was careful to add: "I remain no less in favor of rules, very flexible ones, but rules all the same." In another letter of the same period, he amicably pretended to quarrel with Ernest Raynaud on the prosodic heresies of Le Signe: "Let us rhyme little if we wish, but let us rhyme, so long as we don't exclusively and merely assonate." At an earlier date Verlaine had refrained from following Rimbaud in his revolt against the traditional forms of French poetry. He retains the same wariness, the same discretion with regard to the recklessnesses of the new generation.

After Baju and Décadence, Moréas and the Ecole romane * come to the fore. A new avatar of Verlaine, who once again let himself be drawn in and then, as before, shied away. In 1888 Boulangism is seething. The nationalist thrust is not effective on the political level alone. It gives rise in the world of letters to a powerful movement. The spirit of Decadence, pessimism, and cosmopolitanism is obliged to yield to a new, nationalistic, and determinedly optimistic spirit. No more German philosophy, no more verses laden with obscure intuitions written in disjointed language, but a sharp, clear poetry of strictly French inspiration and qualities. Verlaine let himself be carried along with the current.

A letter he wrote to Cazals in the middle of 1889 describes his new poetic quite clearly. Above all, be clear. One may if really necessary allow a certain amount of blurring, of vagueness, but of a kind that is eventually clear in the context of the whole poem. Effective in any literature, clarity and vigor of style are,

---

* Jean Moréas, himself born in Greece, lead a group of more or less Symbolist poets who in the later 1880's endeavored to draw their symbols from the classical world. [Tr.]

in French literature, indispensable. A frank return to classicism is what is needed: the Romantics were only the French on holiday.

These ideas were unfolding in his mind at the very moment Moréas was bit by bit passing over from symbolism to the *Ecole romane*. One understands, therefore, the verses, imitative of Moréas' Middle Ages style that Verlaine published in his honor in *Cravache* (Horse whip) and *Chat Noir* in 1889. A long piece of verse published two years later in *Plume* and again in a more complete version in *Bonheur* proves that these ideas held the poet's attention from 1889 to 1891. Having thrown over all partisanship, Verlaine returned to truth, to unaffected and actual feeling:

> *L'art tout d'abord doit être et paraître sincère*
> *Et clair absolument: c'est la loi nécessaire*
> *Et dure, n'est-ce pas, les jeunes! mais la loi.*

> Above all art should be and seem sincere
> And absolutely clear: that is the necessary
> And the hard (right, youth!) law—but the law.

He reminds these young writers that he initiated the audacities on which they pride themselves and that, for his part, he now repudiates:

> *Nous, promoteurs de vos, de nos pauvres audaces . . .*

> Us, originators of your, of our poor audacities . . .

The time of scepticism, of derisive laughter, of decadent flourishes, is past. The French must listen to "the blood that courses through [their] veins,"

> *Flux de verve gauloise et flot d'aplomb romain,*
> *Avec, puisqu'un peu Franc, de bon limon germain.*

> Flow of Gallic zest, and tide of Roman poise,
> Alluviate, since somewhat Frank, with good Teutonic loam.

This new *art poétique* appeared on May 15, 1891. At precisely the same time that Charles Maurras published his famous little book on Moréas, in which one may read: The poets "are already dreaming of renewing the ancient Roman synthesis

where Gallic vigor and the tradition of Imperial Rome coexist."
Verlaine's and Maurras' statements correspond point for point.

At this date, however, Verlaine was quarreling with the young
school. He was not invited to the banquet given on February 2,
1891, in Moréas' honor. He wrote to his friend: "Dreadful
young people . . . surround us and as usual do us wrong." A
few days later, he expressed this notion again: "I rather think
we would do well to put these ephebes of rather uninviting mien
down a bit." It was rumored that he had made some insulting
remarks about Moréas; this was doubtless not slander, for at
that same date he wrote with regard to the latter: "He makes
such a fool of himself, he spouts so and stupefies poor boys so
much!" From that time on Verlaine collected, in his *Invectives*
notebook, a certain number of epigrams against his former
friend: he had the good sense, however, or the prudence, not to
publish them.

He had returned to his former solitude. He was aware, from
1890 on, that the young no longer followed him. To Pierre
Louÿs and André Gide, who came to pay him a visit in Broussais, he said in regard to the new poets: "They find me old-
fashioned now."

The Moréas banquet incident in 1891 had confirmed this
impression. He made no effort to get in touch again, and when
in the course of that same year Jules Huret came to question
him for his celebrated interview, Verlaine strongly indicated
his scorn for the agitation of schools of poetry. He declared that
the word "decadent" didn't mean anything, that he did not
understand the word "symbolism," and that when he suffered,
when he enjoyed himself, when he wept, there was nothing
symbolic about it. In his view his contemporaries were only
theoreticians, authors of platforms and manifestoes:

> *Toujours parler et ne jamais chanter,*
> *Grammarien sans cesse à disserter . . .*

> Always talking and never singing,
> Grammarian ceaselessly descanting . . .

he wrote, with Ghil and Moréas, especially, in mind.

He followed his own path. That is, he disengaged himself
little by little from the methods and devices of Decadence and

Symbolism. From 1892 on, the development is clear. And as always with the so-called instinctive, its course is wholly conscious. He writes:

> *Je m'étais éventé dans le Pédant,*
> *Plus que mort, pas né, brume qui se vautre*
> *Aux fondrières d'un art décadent.*

> I went stale with Pedantry,
> More than dead, unborn, a fog wallowing
> In the bogs of decadent art.

His poetry dropped the excessive clevernesses into which it had strayed on more than one occasion. He had the goodness of heart to think that Philomène had helped him bring his poetry back to health:

> *Tu parus! Je naquis sous ta prunelle,*
> *Du sang me battit, de la chair me vint.*

> You appeared! I burgeoned 'neath your gaze,
> Blood throbbed in me, I took on flesh.

To disregard these statements, one must be blind to the way in which they are confirmed by study of Verlaine's last works. He is now weary of "things attempted in some dim yesteryear"; he listens to those inner voices, now restored, that had once inspired his masterpieces:

> *Je fais ces vers comme on marche devant soi,*
> *—Sans muser, sans flâner, sans se distraire aux choses*
> *De la route.*

> I make these lines as one walks ahead
> —Without browsing, or dawdling, or diverting oneself with the
>   things
> Along the way.

It was a Verlaine liberated at last that death silenced in 1896.

AFTER SAGESSE

Encouraged by the reception he had met, Verlaine, in 1883, set about writing several books at once. He worked on his *Poèmes de jadis et de naguère* (Poems of Yesteryear and Yesterday), on his *Mémoires d'un veuf* (Memoirs of a Widower), and on the collection *Amour*. He published quite a number of poems in magazines. In 1884, he succeeded in having Vanier publish the first of the three projected volumes, to which he gave the abbreviated title of *Jadis et naguère*.

In all this activity one should establish a few distinctions: Verlaine is practically emptying his desk drawers. To be more precise, he is drawing on the large black trunk that he has carried about with him for nine years through his innumerable changes of residence and which, at one time, he had believed lost. He sends some of this work to magazines; some of the poems printed in *Jadis et naguère* date from before the war. In the new volume one finds poems that had appeared in *Hanneton* in 1867, leavings from the *Les Vaincus* volume he had been working on as early as 1869 and to which he had returned in 1873, parts of *Cellulairement* that had not been collected in *Sagesse*, a few "In the style of . . ." pieces, and the diabolical tales that may have been written in Brussels.

But aside from the revival of these old works there were, among the pieces printed in magazines, recent compositions which would soon find their way into *Amour* and *Parallèlement*. It is these latter that enable one to trace the direction Verlaine is taking.

It may seem paradoxical to find in these often savage pieces a hint of spirituality. One should read, however, the most brazen of these, the "Lunes" (Moons) series, or "Limbes" (Limbo) or "Lombes" (Loins) in *Parallèlement*, or again, the "Ballade de la mauvaise réputation" (Ballad of Bad Reputation). The poem does not conceal his debasement. He jeers at the innocence of *Fêtes galantes*. Within this wretchedness, however, burns a flame. Underneath these pitiful or shameful guises we detect love. For this is not the mean or the "norm." It is the gruesomeness of stage sets, of necessities submitted to. And it is for that reason pure in the midst of the worst kinds of degradation.

This is what young writers of 1883–1884 could find in Verlaine's most recent publications. The very form of his poems marvelously reflected their inspiration. Subtle and compact, often obscure. Expressing through bold ellipses the tension between that purity and those lapses. Wrapped in mystery and doing nothing to clear it up. Endeavoring through the most subtle possible play of internal rhyme and assonance to give a direct and evocative rendering of those leaps, those falls, those gropings.

Too much imbued with the delicious music of the early collections, the present-day reader tends to neglect these works of the second period. To get an idea of their greatness, he should read those books of the same period in which others attempted to convey modern sensibility. Aside from Laforgue, how heavy, on the one hand, their fashionable melancholies, and on the other, their "neuroses," when compared with the biting, profound, and brave confessions of the "exhausted prowler."

THE TRILOGY OF GRACE

If there is one fact that prevents maintaining the traditional image of a Verlaine drifting at random, if there is one certain proof of his lucidity, of the breadth and strength of his schemes, it is the project, conceived around 1885 and finally carried out, of two great symmetrical ensembles, one of which was to sing of the call of divine love and the other to describe the exigencies and follies of sensual desire. The first panel of this diptych was conceived as a sequel to *Sagesse*. Together with this masterwork which was already published, *Amour* and *Bonheur* comprise the Trilogy of Grace, and Verlaine had time to cap this ensemble with *Liturgies intimes* (Inner Devotions). The second panel includes those five collections published in Verlaine's lifetime, *Parallèlement*, *Chansons pour elle* (Songs for Her), *Odes en son honneur* (Odes in Her Honor), *Elégies* (Elegies), and *Dans les Limbes* (In Limbo), plus a sixth, *Chair* (Flesh), which came out after his death. As if so many volumes were not sufficient, Verlaine published, marginal to the major work, a number of collections of amicable and satirical pieces addressed both to friends and to people he didn't like. *Dédicaces* (Dedications) and *Epigrammes* (Epigrams) appeared before his death. *Invectives* was published later, through the indiscretion of his friend and publisher Léon Vanier.

It is customary to pass quickly over these works of his last years. Perhaps, however, they have more value than people say

At any rate it is perfectly proper not to accept without verification an overall judgment that treats with equal disdain ten years of the work of a great poet. Historical impartiality requires that one take a closer look.

Since 1875, Verlaine had dreamed of publishing a volume that he wished to call *Amour*. He devoted the first months of 1887 to moulding and finishing it. The book was still not published in October, and the poet took this opportunity to polish and revise his poems. In January 1888, he sent the last poems to Vanier, and the book came out a short time before March 26.

Amour, to his mind, was to be a kind of continuation and extension of *Sagesse.* It was to show the place that love had occupied in his life. Cause of his misfortunes, source of his redemption, it was the secret law responsible for the true grandeur of life. This idea gives the book unity despite the variety of recollections that are called up. For here, as in *Sagesse,* Verlaine brings together pieces that extend over a period of more than ten years. One finds poems from 1875 that relate remembrances of prison, and others that were written in Bournemouth in 1877. And one finds, especially, the admirable "Lamento pour Lucien Létinois" (Lament for Lucien Létinois).

Those who remain unmoved by this poetry of purity, tenderness, and resignation are to be pitied. Beneath the hand of God great and terrible, Verlaine bows his head. He knows he has no right, here on earth, to happiness, that the joy he found during the four years he spent near Lucien was a gratuitous and revocable gift. God took his comrade back. He bows his head and worships. And further, he asks if he has not deserved his misfortune. For had he the right to take Lucien away from the obscure and peaceful life he was leading and draw him into his own adventures? And in his extreme happiness, had he not forgotten Him who had given him Lucien?

Poetry of humble submission. But poetry, too, of purity. Everything in these beautiful poems becomes suspect and distressing if one supposes for a moment that they are founded on deceit. But they themselves contain evidence that does not lie. If it is wise to be wary of defenders of Verlaine, it is impossible to mistake the involuntary affirmation, the implicit declaration that emerges from his poems, the atmosphere of joyous and childlike purity, the Eden-like atmosphere in which they are steeped.

Verlaine was an adventurer in love; that is the idea implicit in the whole collection:

J'ai la fureur d'aimer. Mon coeur si faible est fou.

I am infected with love's frenzy. My poor weak heart is mad.

His past misfortunes were born of that frenzy, that madness. When the call of love sounds within him, he throws himself into the breach without thinking, without looking ahead. There was his love for Rimbaud—which he recalls in one word. There was his love for Lucien. There were, and will be, others. Weakness, one says. But why not rather say, irresistible force and power of desire?

Je suis dur comme un juif et têtu comme lui.

I'm as tough and as stubborn as a Jew.

Amour is a tough and forceful book. It has its faults. It is sometimes overelaborate, excessively clever, pedantic. But, on the other hand, how many beauties! What an attempt at innovation, what determination to find a tone, to create a style, to achieve hitherto unknown effects! One figure from the past inspires Verlaine: Villon. He wants to be the Villon of the end of his century. That is why he writes ballads and employs a discreetly archaic language. Christian poet, man of the Middle Ages strayed into the sad times in which we live, he continues to have recourse to allegory. Moral life presents itself to his mind in the guise of entities that have their source, one might say, in the *Roman de la Rose* (Romance of the Rose). He is in pursuit of Happiness, but he has found nothing but Error in his path; Pride has clipped his wings. A questionable enterprise, doubtless, as is any return to the past. But not one to be scorned, for in the case of this poet it is less a matter of carrying on a dead tradition than of reviving an ancient form of beauty.

Rather than over these attempts, however interesting, one should pause, in *Amour*, over what it offers that is unquestionably totally new. And that is, to begin with, an art of description very far removed from the methods of impressionism. The beautiful poem, "Bournemouth," for instance, contains none of the

juxtaposed notations dear to the Goncourt brothers. It is dominated rather by the humble worship of beauty. Landscape is no
longer a plethora of colors, but a harmony presented to the poet;
and it is this harmony he concentrates on. Whence the pre-
dominance, in his depiction, of essential values, and the care
taken to establish their relationships. One quotation is sufficient:

> *Il fait un de ces temps ainsi que je les aime,*
> *Ni brume, ni soleil! le soleil deviné,*
> *Pressenti, du brouillard mourant dansant à même*
> *Le ciel très haut qui tourne et fuit, rose de crème;*
> *L'atmosphère est de perle et la mer d'or fané.*

> This is a kind of weather I like,
> Neither fog, nor sun! the sun surmised,
> Sensed, fading haze dancing up very high
> In the sky, which eddies and runs, creamy-rose;
> The air is pearl and the sea fretted gold.

The beauty of "Paysages belges" is here perhaps surpassed.
One admires too, especially in the *lamento*, a style, in the real
sense of the word—that is, the expression of an interior vision.
The poet managed to find the rhythms, sonorities, and the
images to convey all the purity of his love for Lucien, the unreal
ingenuousness of the dream he nourished for four years. It is not
our intellect he reaches and convinces. It is our sensibility. It
vibrates at the pitch he intends, entirely imbued with the
flowing limpidity of these poems, wholly bathed in their light.

Even before *Amour* had come out, Verlaine was already preparing the third volume of his trilogy—*Bonheur*. He worked on
it during the whole month of May 1887. By August this collection already contained a dozen poems. But during the following
autumn and winter, the poet's attention turned in other direc-
tions. He hardly gave *Bonheur* a thought throughout the year
1888. At intervals, however, he wrote a new poem which he set
aside to fill out this collection. It was not until the end of 1889
that he came back to it with the firm intention of finishing it
quickly. He wrote five new poems. He considered it done. But
circumstances delayed publication, and during the year 1890, the
volume was further augmented. It finally appeared in June
1891.

Ripened slowly over a period of four years, *Bonheur* was to be the crowning work of the Christian trilogy. It was a sound idea. *Amour* had expressed the leap toward spiritual love of a soul that was still all aquiver. *Bonheur* was meant to express the assuagement, the peacefulness of the soul within a ruined body. It was to convey the plenitude that is born of equilibrium finally achieved. But the work lacked the necessary coherence. Too many of the poems stop by the way to abuse Mathilde and to maintain that she is responsible for the distress that engulfs the poet. To be fair, from the point of view of poetry alone, certain of these diatribes have, for all their unjustness, a kind of savage grandeur that is not without its beauty. But what is intolerable are those poems in which Verlaine beats his breast, confesses himself a poor sinner, and then, immediately thereafter, avoids naming any real and specific grounds for complaint. These Tartuffe-like posturings are reflected in the quality of the language, make it fumbling and shifty to the point of pompous nonsense.

But just when one is on the point of closing the book, certain poems show the continuing presence of superior powers. Once Verlaine refrains from pleading and preaching, when he recalls his lapses and his efforts at rectification, when he evokes in a few elevated stanzas yuletide nights and glowing Christmas Eves, we are once more in the presence of the author of *Sagesse*. He has overwhelming outcries of remorse and despair, outcries that have no equal in authenticity other than in certain of those Psalms of which he, better than anyone, understood the pathos. In describing the bare altar of Good Friday or the mournfulness of Allhallows Eves or the simple ceremonies of a country church, he strikes a tone in which simplicity, fineness of execution, and feeling are combined in a delightful and forceful manner. These poems enable us to understand the meaning Christian life had for Verlaine: a life of wisdom and purity, stamped with the beauty of old forms of worship and punctuated by feast days that gave it rhythm and meaning.

An uneven collection, consequently. But on the whole a great book. In the poems of lesser quality, the badness does not come from lack of talent but from pushing poetry beyond its limits—with resultant overstraining and overartfulness. Verlaine spoke of *Bonheur* on two occasions, once to W. G. C. Byvanck in 1891,

and again to André Gide and Pierre Louÿs who had come to pay
him a visit. With all three men he used the same phrase to describe his book: it's a strong book. "It is not an easy book to
read," he said to W. G. C. Byvanck. "One feels that life has
passed through it." And more emphatically, to Gide and Louÿs:
"*Bonheur* will be a strong book. Its happiness will not seem very
happy." That is what the poet wanted to make us feel in his
book. And that is what, to a very high degree, he managed to do.

In publishing *Bonheur* Verlaine narrowly missed abandoning
his friend Léon Vanier. In 1888, Huysmans and Léon Bloy had
put him in touch with Albert Savine. On September 15, 1888,
the poet signed a contract that bound him to bring out *Bonheur*
with his new publisher. He immediately drew advances on his
future royalties. In 1891, however, Léon Vanier was able to
prove to him that he was not free to part company with him;
the two publishers reached an agreement, Albeit Savine re-
covered his investment, and *Bonheur* was published under the
Vanier imprint.

The slim volume of *Liturgies intimes* appeared in March
1892. It is not on the same level as the great Christian trilogy.
It is a work of particular intent and meant for a special audience.
Verlaine was in friendly communication with Emmanuel Sig-
noret. The latter had undertaken publication of *Le Saint-Graal*
(The Holy Grail), a Catholic youth magazine. He asked
Verlaine to lend a hand. The *Liturgies* were created especially
for the *Saint-Graal* readership. They were, moreover, made up
of poems of various dates. One of them goes back as far as 1878,
and it has been shown above that Verlaine, as early as *Bonheur*,
had applied himself to celebrating certain of the beauties of the
Catholic liturgy.

This volume gives a curious impression. It contains some of
the author's worst poems. Pompous nonsense. Literal translations of liturgical texts with ridiculous results. One of the stran-
gest of these is doubtless:

> *Il engendra, ne fit pas Jésus-Christ* . . .
>
> He begot, did not make Jesus Christ . . .

which is both a direct and ludicrous translation of *Genitum,
non factum* from the Nicene Creed. Verlaine's mistake, here

as elsewhere, but even more here, is giving in to his old penchant for the didactic. A comparison of two other poems from the *Liturgies* convinces one of his error. First, the one in which he expounds an idea in the abstract:

> *Sécheresse maligne et coupable langueur,*
> *Il n'est remède encore à vos tristesses noires*
> *Que telles dévotions surérogatoires*
> *Comme des mois de Marie et du Sacré-Coeur.*

> Evil aridity and culpable inertia,
> There is but one cure for your dark depressions
> Such supererogatory devotions
> As months of Mary and the Sacred Heart.

And secondly, the one in which the poet lets loose a flood of images charged with significance:

> *L'agneau cherche l'amère bruyère.*
> *C'est le sel et non le sucre qu'il préfère.*
> *Son pas fait le bruit d'une averse sur la poussière.*

> The lamb seeks out the bitter heather.
> It's salt, not sugar, he prefers.
> His step makes the sound of a shower on powder.

Two "systems": two effects!

Poetry, then, does not play Verlaine false. *Liturgies intimes* contains some very beautiful poems—"Rois" (Kings), for instance, and even better, "Juin" (June). The poem on the office of compline has a hidden beauty which those who are acquainted with the richness of this evening rite will appreciate. Who knows but what this humble collection carries a kind of message for the poetry of the future? "Vêpres rustiques" (Country Vespers) prefigures in astonishingly precise fashion the style, imagery, and rhythm of Francis Jammes's Christian writings. "Circoncision" (Circumcision) is not a good poem, but the thirteen-syllable line with its elusive caesuras encourage one to consider the short distance between it and Claudel's verse form. In a number of places Verlaine obtains from the couplet powerful effects of chanted litany and broken supplication.

The same burden has been laid on these four religiously inspired collections as on *Sagesse*. And with stronger arguments. Many do not care to believe in the sincerity of a Christian poet whose personal behavior is so scandalous. Even those who are

willing to admit that the author of *Sagesse* was still a believer
when he published his masterpiece are not convinced that he
was one still at the time of *Amour*, *Bonheur*, and *Liturgies intimes*.

The most trustworthy records, however, leave no doubt. He
was still a true Christian at the time. Letters of 1887 and 1889
inform us that he attended Mass and Sunday vespers regularly,
and that he kneeled at the foot of his bed every morning and
every evening to say his prayers. It is true that he had periods
of despondency. He told Byvanck in 1891: "It has been more
than a year now that I have not dared to go to Communion."
But who could mistake this feeling of his own unworthiness
for apathy or skepticism?

He is not only a practicing Catholic. He is a believer, and a
strictly orthodox one. He believes in the "flashing insights" of
Catholicism, and in the "interesting refutations" that apologetics
opposes to science. He has constructed a kind of religious metaphysic, an overall view of the world and of man, entirely inspired
by the religious spirit. The almost carnal and palpable presence
of God supremely realized in the Eucharist. Man's life stirred
by love, thrown into adventure by it, running the risk of sin and
damnation, but saved by spiritual love. Catholic liturgy, the
expression of that religious metaphysic, conveying its rich and
moving poetry. And finally, the complete assimilation of that
which is created into the divine. Verlaine said one curiously profound thing in his conversation with André Gide and Pierre
Louÿs. The lesson of *Bonheur*, he said, is that there is but one
true happiness: and that is knowing that God exists. At the
risk of seeming pedantic, one might say that Verlaine went as
far as that theocentrism wherein Abbé Brémond saw the true
essence of religious feeling.

It would take the meeting with Eugénie Krantz in 1891, the
reawakening of carnal frenzies, the plunge into the nether
world, to dim in Verlaine's soul a light that, since *Sagesse* and
despite appearances, had never ceased to shine.

THE POETRY OF SENSUAL LOVE

In October 1885, Verlaine had announced that the *Amour*
and *Bonheur* sequences were to be followed by another work,

and that he was preparing some "sinful volumes." These were to bear the overall title of *Parallèlement*. He later decided to give this title to the first volume of the series alone. This collection, long in the making, came out in July 1889.

In this book he chose to celebrate in the crudest possible fashion the pleasures of the flesh. *Parallèlement* is a disgraceful book. It brings together both old and recent poems which have, with very few exceptions, the common feature of speaking shamelessly of the most sensual kind of love. Poems about Mathilde, poems in which the distant figure of Rimbaud looms up once more, poems inspired by the filthy debaucheries at Coulommes, and finally, lines in celebration of the women whose easy favors Verlaine had received.

But how flavorful this collection is! Rather than the frosty obscenities of the eighteenth century, it makes one think of Ronsard's *Fôlatries* (Frolics) and the uncensored collections of Theophilus' time. It would be hypocritical or blind to deny the fire and dash of the series "Filles" (Girls), and with it the poetic value of these very beautiful poems.

There is, however, something even more important to be noted. And that is that the distance between *Amour* and *Parallèlement* is not so great as one might think at first glance. Verlaine thought it would be amusing to present these two collections as *parallels* of one another, and the success of his title with the public proves he was right. It is, nonetheless, a superficial notion. If it is true that his life at that time was unfolding on two parallel levels, it is true only in the area of assumed attitudes. The two levels have a common basis. It is that obscure and powerful impulse, that desire of making himself welcomed and loved by all. And Verlaine is quite aware of it. Old faun with pricked-up ears, he goes sniffing through the world, bent on the beauty it offers, greedy to taste its every fruit. Remorselessly, for he could never imagine that pleasure should ever offer itself to him without his having the right to take it. But alert too to more elevated impulses, ready to perish with love before the figure of Christ or that of the Virgin, which he responds to in his innermost self, completely open to that supreme love he calls God.

Verlaine once wrote to Félicien Rops: *Parallèlement* is a book that is "more *bitter* and *tough* than sensual." It is, indeed, a good deal more instinctive than considered, and is less expressive of complaisance with sin than of acceptance of adventure, with its known measure of misery and catastrophe. As an admirer of Barbey d'Aurevilly, Verlaine detests Protestantism, Jansenism, all casts of mind that, in the name of morality, surround human life with barriers and fences. He is quite prepared, as was the author of *Prophètes du passé*, to say that his broad, inclusive, ample Catholicism "embraces human nature wholly," and that it is willing to go as low as the dual cesspool of man—the heart, and even the loins!

Parallèlement was a very free book but was not lewd to the degree punishable by law. Verlaine brought together the bolder pieces in a little volume that was published clandestinely in 1890. It bears the title *Femmes* (Women). It has come to light from a letter not collected in the *Correspondance* that the poet had arranged for its publication with Kistemackers, the well-known Belgian house. Bibliographers consider it a truism that the poems in *Femmes* were composed a good many years before 1890. One readily believes them. However, the only poems that are dated are marked 1889–1890, and the similarity between the poems in this collection and those of recent composition in *Parallèlement* is great.

Somewhat later, in 1892, Verlaine planned, for publication by Vanier, another collection—a sequel to *Femmes*—the title and subject of which was *Hombres* (Men). This book was never published during his lifetime. For whatever conclusion one may wish to draw about Verlaine's personal life in 1891, most of the poems in this obscene collection are dated that year.

At that time, however, he had just become intimate and had practically set up housekeeping with Eugénie Krantz, and this relationship inspired the *Chansons pour elle*. They were published at the end of 1891, and it is probable that the poems that make up this collection were written during the course of the preceding months. Thus Eugénie inspired, if not the whole, at least the greater portion of this volume. That is probably what explains the indecency of these poems in which immorality is shamelessly acknowledged. Verlaine had no illusions about this woman. She is a shrew, a liar, and sometimes forgets herself so far as to strike him. But he forgives her everything because he is old, because he is afraid of not having a roof over his head and of being left alone, and because Eugénie gives him certain joys, the only ones left within his grasp. In this poverty-crushed man life assumes the lowly forms of animality. Small scruples and the common decencies are considered an indulgence and ignored. Verlaine has let drop the cloak of hypocrisy which his destitute condition will no longer suffer. So much so, he says,

> *Si bien qu'il est très bien de faire comme font*
> *Les bonnes bêtes de la terre.*
>
> So much so that it's very good to do as do
> The good beasts of the earth.

One would have to lack all sympathy for certain kinds of moral failure to be merely indignant or scornful about this. Yet if one focuses on the poetic value alone of *Chansons pour elle*, one cannot but confess that such elemental spiritual states, such lifeless and unqualified degradation can only with difficulty become the object of poetry. After one has appreciated in a few scattered poems a little—very little—of that zest which enlivened, in *Parallèlement*, the flavorful "Filles" series, after one has drawn from the volume as a whole a pitiful impression of physical and moral wretchedness, there is nothing more to be said.

Perhaps, however, one should observe that certain rhythms, certain repeated refrains that seem unpleasant or ridiculous seem more justifiable if one recalls that these poems are meant to be songs. One might be less hard on this poor book if one took into account the fact that Verlaine hoped to attract the attention of musicians, and that he deliberately set himself to write at the level of the cabaret song. Whence the overly facile forms, the prettinesses so completely alien to his talent. When he wrote:

> *Es-tu brune ou blonde?*
> *Sont-ils noirs ou bleus,*
>   *Tes yeux?*
>
> Are you dark or are you light?
> Are your eyes
>   Black or bright?

he had a sorry excuse: he was composing the verses of a "song."

Chansons pour elle had not yet been put together in a book when Verlaine wrote the *Odes en son honneur*. On November

12, 1891, he informed Vanier that they were "progressing," and
toward the end of December he had already put together a group
of six hundred lines. He thereafter considered them ready for
print; but as was his custom he continued to "enlarge" on them
throughout the following year. It was not until May 1893 that
they appeared in the bookstores.

It is generally acknowledged that they were written for
Eugénie. During the period in which they were composed, however, Verlaine, as we have seen, was divided between his "wives."
Certain poems, in fact, seem clearer if taken as addressed to
Philomène rather than her rival. The allusion to a saint, a virgin,
and a martyr brings Saint Philomena to mind, and the one place
in which the addressee is called by name, it is the name Philomène the poet utters.

Odes en son honneur should not be confused with *Chansons
pour elle*. Had the poet's energy revived? Did this subject inspire him in more felicitous fashion? The *odes* are indisputably
much superior to the *chansons*. Certain poems celebrate the
beauties of woman in coarse terms. But they do so with more
warmth and zest, in a tone that recalls the good poems in
Parallèlement.

They do not, moreover, give the collection its dominant tone.
More often, Verlaine evokes the unhappy past of the woman
who now joins her miseries with his own. He does not neglect
the fact that she once had her share of happiness, and that her
present fall is thereby harder to endure. But she is brave and
cheerful. Her life was an adventure. She ran life's risks with
high daring; she failed. Society scorns her, as she scorns Verlaine.
The latter feels pity and respect for this wounded Amazon. This
very humane note alone would suffice to give the *odes* a quality
the *chansons* lack.

But they have another, more strictly poetic quality and merit
close examination. They have a firmness of touch, the sentences
show a quickness of line that is altogether extraordinary, and
that one would value even more highly if they did not suffer
by comparison with earlier masterpieces. They are, however, of
the same order as the latter. The line is still, or better, is again,
"the soaring thing"—completely resonant and springing. Sometimes it is used merely to express trivial commonplaces, and

sometimes these remain so opaque and heavy that the jet dies down. But we should remember that all poetry lies, not in the character of the things observed, but in a quality of vision. Verlaine's once again hit (more than once in the *odes*) upon the lovely freshness of earlier days. The poet was quite aware of this. He was an unerring judge of the worth of his books. The *Odes en son honneur*, he said to Vanier, is both more substantial and more weighty, but especially "better written" than the *Chansons pour elle*.

In the same month as the *Odes en son honneur*, May 1893, Verlaine brought out a volume of *Elégies*. This was an old plan he was now executing. In October 1887, he had asked Jules Tellier for a Latin-French Catullus, Tibullus, and Propertius, and had confided to several people his long-cherished ambition of translating Ovid into French. *Elégies* was born of this old ambition, and nothing could be more superficial than seeing it as an undertaking written merely to bring in "some cash." He wrote the elegies during the second half of 1892, and some of them appeared in *Echo de Paris* in September and October.

As, alas, almost all of the collections of this period, *Elégies* presents poems of very uneven value. It isn't altogether that Verlaine has become careless: his scruples as an artist have, basically, lost none of their strictness. And it is not exactly that his inspiration is wearing thin; he is still full of energy, rich in ideas and images. But he too often assumes that "clown" pose he himself admitted to—and at such times his mockings, his display of degradation, his willingness to put up with things ignoble, affect his art, make his sentences knotty, and cloud the purity of his language. However, if one sets aside the few elegies in which he gives in to this temptation, the remainder of the collection has a genuine and affecting beauty. How can one possibly speak of Coppée here? Beneath the simplicity of tone— intentional with the poet because he believes it is essential to the Tibullian elegy—one must appreciate the powerful rhythm, the variety of line lengths, the impression of amplitude the poem very often yields. What puts so many critics off is not, as they think, the poetic interest of the collection, its artistic value, but its setting. The pitiful setting of jealous crises, shameful recon- ciliations—all that, doubtless without their being aware of it, obscures for them the exquisite skill of language and line, the persistence in the poet of that sensibility they admire in the major collections. They do not see the courage and daring of the poet's attempt, of his effort to describe a life from which, one by one, all the refinements, all the comforts too, with which civilization overlays and sheathes the plain and brutish gestures of primitive man, have been stripped. They are deaf to this sorrowing song, this appeal that arises from the depths of wretchedness and from the yearning for a world of peace, of dignity achieved, and purity.

In October 1892, Verlaine was in Broussais. He considered *Elégies* finished. He started a new collection which he called *Dans les Limbes* (In Limbo). A letter written to Léon Vanier proves that he had at that time a clear idea of what he wanted to do: describe his present condition of hospitalized invalid, his ideas, which had taken a more somber turn of late, and his hopes for recovery. In December 1892, he sent the first hundred lines to his publisher, and on January 13, 1893, he considered the volume of four hundred and fifty lines finished.

Several features determine the cast of this collection. It is not only more sober and chaste, it is more Christian than preceding volumes. One guesses that the woman who comes to visit him in the hospital and for whom he writes these poems is no longer Eugénie the heathen, but Philomène, who encourages the poet in his religious impulses. That is undoubtedly what explains the greater elevation of this collection. Verlaine's love for this woman is not free of miseries. She too is sometimes quarrelsome and violent. But when she is in good humor, she has a cheerfulness over an undercurrent of melancholy, and susceptibilities that save their relationship from being altogether distasteful. She can be sweet and charming to the poor old man whom she calls "the Devil Himself." Her visits bring the invalid joy and hope for a better future. These are the major themes of the book.

On July 3, 1893, once again in Broussais, Verlaine added a preface to this book. In it he announced the end of this series, of which he had grown weary. He pointed out the new tone of the poems in the book, the evening calm that inspired them, the advent of a major change in himself to be discerned in them.

The manuscript then remained in his drawer for nearly a whole year. The book was not published until May 1894.

At this date Verlaine was already working on a number of other poems that were an open return to the sensualities of the *Chansons pour elle*. They were published after the poet's death in a collection that bears the title *Chair* (Flesh). Then, between July and November 1893, he wrote the poems that today comprise his *Livre posthume* (Posthumous Book). He hoped to have it published, despite the title, before his death. At one time he foresaw publication for the month of October 1895. He died before this plan was effected. *Livre posthume*, as it stands, represents only a portion of a much broader work whose sources are still difficult to determine. But it is more important to discover Verlaine's effort in the work as it now stands, his attempt, during the second half of 1893, at atonement, rather than to try to follow the successive gropings of the poet.

For almost all of the poems in *Livre posthume* are beautiful and moving. The love expressed in them is no longer the sensual love of *Chansons pour elle*. It is the union of two lives, joined for better or for worse, dignified by the notion of duration beyond the grave. Restored to life after the terrible ordeal of July, the poet speaks as a man who has seen death face to face and has not forgotten the encounter. Whence a solemnity, an unexpected depth of resonance. And at the same time, not less refined, but more direct forms, the disappearance of those sometimes unendurable mumblings that cluttered up the volumes of the preceding period.

In considering the collections of divine love and the poems of carnal love as a whole and in sequence, two observations must be made. We realize first of all that these two allegedly parallel series were written at different times. When, at the beginning of 1892, his *Liturgies intimes* closes the series of religious poems, Verlaine had published only *Parallèlement* and *Chansons pour elle*. He was working on the *Odes en son honneur,* which did not come out until 1893. *Elégies, Dans les Limbes, Livre posthume,* and *Chair* were yet unwritten and unpublished. One sees from this the degree to which the notion of parallel composition of these two series requires explication and reservations.

We have established, on the other hand, that far from answering to an oversimple picture of a total and permanent lapse, these collections of the last period trace a development in Verlaine's poetic conceptions and show, from 1892 on, a definite rise in the quality of his works. We have seen above that Verlaine, in 1892, wrenched himself free "of the bogs of decadent art," declared that he was weary "of things attempted in some dim yesteryear," proclaimed his joy at being reborn, at coming out of the mists, at creating works in which the blood runs clear and warm. Reading *Chair* and reading *Livre posthume* convinces one of this return to vigor in those very years that have traditionally been thought to be the last stages of decay.

OTHER COLLECTIONS

In November 1888, Verlaine considered taking a few of the poems out of *Parallèlement* and putting them together under a new title, *Amis* (Men Friends), as a recollection of the earlier *Amies* (Girl Friends) but with an entirely different moral intent. In June 1889, this plan took shape in his mind, but he wavered between two titles, *Amis* and *Dédicaces*. He finally decided on the latter. In October he turned over the manuscript to his friend Léon Deschamps, director of *Plume*, and the work came out in book form in March 1890. At that time it contained only forty-one poems. Four years later a second printing of a considerably enlarged version containing one hundred and nine poems was made.

A dazzling volume, even in its debatable parts. It has a variety of accent, it shows a flexibility of talent that is quite proof enough of the lack of truth in the alleged barrenness of the aged poet. It has been said that several poems were written only to acknowledge certain favors bestowed upon him. This is saddening but not difficult to believe. Certain minor poems in *Dédicaces* can hardly be explained otherwise. Others, which at first glance seem curiously awkward, are actually parodies in which the poet amuses himself by adopting the style and reproducing the tics of the persons to whom the lines are addressed. For in this fertile volume, Verlaine assumes all possible tones. One finds malice, good humor, sadness. He makes fun of all styles: Villon, Corneille, the moderns. Sometimes some of the most beautiful lines he ever wrote spring forth—those, for

instance, inspired by Villier's death, and Rimbaud's. All kinds
of feelings all jumbled together; sometimes a voluptuousness
not unlike that of certain poems in *Chansons pour elle,* and
sometimes the chasteness of certain solemn and spiritual friendships. *Dédicaces* is both a priceless record of this rich and tortured and contradictory soul, and a great work of art.

The Preface to *Chair,* which came out in May 1894, was
dated July 3, 1873, and announced a profound transformation
in Verlaine's soul. "The calm of eventide," he wrote. This is the
same thought that appeared in 1894 in the delightful volume of
Epigrammes.

It is important to see clearly what this means. This is a new
Verlaine declaring himself. His passions are silenced. Even his
mystic ardors are subdued. Is he still a believer? Yes, but with
a faith that has hardly any resemblance to the strong convictions
of earlier days. A wisdom rather, a very subdued feeling, in the
midst of the doubts that have come back. "Extreme views" are
part of the past. Similarly, the development of ideas about
poetry. Return to the old doctrine of Art for Art's Sake. Art is a
game, and Verlaine returns to it. He will be the good canon of
Parnasse.

A step backward, some will say, one that indicates final ex-
haustion. But why not call it rather: serenity, new breadth of
outlook, the lucidity of a subdued and chastened spirit? He looks
with indulgence on the agitations of the young. He understands
their audacity. He is not disturbed to see them all worked up over
Ibsen or Schopenhauer. But he remains on the sidelines. *Epigrammes* is not confined just to invoking older forms of poetry.
The poems very clearly recall the luminous and pure artistry of
Fêtes galantes. Two lines express the poet's intent, his cast of
mind, the impression this collection gives:

> *Il ne me faut plus qu'un air de flûte*
> *Très lointain en des couchants éteints . . .*
>
> I need now only a strain of flute
> Far off in sunsets that have set . . .

That is the Verlaine of 1894.

Epigrammes came out, as listed in the *Journal de la Librairie*
(The Bookseller), on December 15, 1894, but it is said that

the book was on sale from the preceding August on. This was the last work Verlaine himself had published. At the time he had two other collections—*Chair* and *Varia*—in hand. He died before having them published.

We have seen of what *Chair* consisted, and that it was comprised mainly of poems of sensual love written in 1894. The *Varia* collection was planned on a broader scale. The poet had been thinking about it since 1893, and one may assume that he intended to assemble therein numerous poems from all periods of his life. As presented by his first editor, it contains mainly poems from 1893 and 1894: recollections of trips to England and Holland, of his illness in July 1893, of hospitals, of poverty and of quarrels in the furnished rooms where the poor old man confronted his furies. But in all this an artistry that becomes simpler, tighter, purer. A poetry that is about to get away from, or actually does get away from, the mumblings of his bad period. Such a poem as "Ex imo," which was inspired by the crisis of July 1893 and the reawakening of old passions, would not be unworthy of *Sagesse*:

> O Jésus, vous m'avez puni moralement
> Quand j'étais digne encor d'une noble souffrance.
> Maintenant que mes torts ont dépassé l'outrance,
> O Jésus, vous me punissez physiquement.

> O Jesus, you punished me morally
> When I was still worthy of lofty pain
> Now that my wrongs have passed all restraint,
> O Jesus, you punish me physically.

The impression that emerges from the *Varia* poems confirms and reinforces that of *Epigrammes* and *Livre posthume*.

Eighteen months after Verlaine's death Léon Vanier published a volume titled *Invectives*. Squeamish souls deplored this publication, claimed that Verlaine would have disapproved of it, and accused the publisher of being indiscreet and greedy for profit. But there is no doubt that Verlaine envisaged and desired the publication of the book. He was already working on it in 1891. He had outlined its contents and had already drawn some money as an advance on royalties.

As one might expect, this book contains some of the best and some of the worst of Verlaine—some poems that are full of verve or magnificently angry, and others that are lamentably platitudinous or clumsy. How could one possibly call *Invectives* a book devoid of interest? The poet's antipathies, rancors, ire help us grasp a whole side of his character: the brutal candor of his views, his pride, that of a man ruined but still on his feet, his contempt for false values. They also enable us better to understand the position he took in the literary controversies of his time, amidst the Symbolists, the *Ecole romane*, and Decadents, who tore each other to pieces as he looked on amused. Whatever some people have thought, something would be lacking in our knowledge of the man and of his talent if we did not have *Invectives*.

THE PROSE WORKS

During his entire career as a writer Verlaine dreamed of composing works in prose—novels, short stories, critical studies. He even considered writing plays. But of all these projects, few were realized.

Previous to 1870, Verlaine contributed to a number of different magazines studies on Barbey d'Aurevilly, Baudelaire, and Coppée that remain important to this day. They owe a great deal to the admirable prose pieces in Baudelaire's *Petits Poèmes en prose* and in his *Art romantique* (Romantic Art). He assimilated the doctrine of the man who was at that time his mentor. He even adopted his tone, the flow, the rhythm of his sentences. He who will soon create a prose of his own, one that is colorful and polished yet relaxed almost to the point of seeming careless, does his utmost in these essays to match the compactness and the haughty, cutting manner of his model.

At this same time he was publishing some short prose poems, "Le Corbillard" (The Hearse), "Mal'aria" (Evil Melody), "Nevermore," and others that he will later include in *Mémoires d'un veuf*. He even took it upon himself to contribute a fantastic tale, *Le Poteau* (The Post), to *Hanneton* in 1867. One detects in these prose pieces the macabre humor, the ironical melancholy that is reflected in *Poèmes saturniens*. He undoubtedly had Baudelaire's *Petits Poèmes en prose* in mind. But to understand how much Verlaine's sensibility differed from Baudelaire's, one should read "Les Fleurs artificielles" (Artificial

Flowers) which appeared in *Parodie* in January 1870. An eminently Baudelairian theme; the taste for the artificial, the unusual, the strange. But all that remains of this in Verlaine are a lot of dainty reflections upon the humble cloth flowers that decorate the hats of nice young working girls and elderly maiden ladies of wounded heart!

From the period following his conversion we have one posthumously published piece, *Voyage en France par un Français* (Travels in France by a Frenchman). Written in its present-day form in 1880, it remained unpublished for a long time because, we are told, no publisher would run the risk of putting out this furious diatribe against the modern mind and the Republic. Verlaine shows himself, at this date, to be a disciple of Joseph de Maistre, Barbey d'Aurevilly, and probably Veuillot. He borrows from them the general views on French history which, since De Maistre's *Les Soirées de Saint-Pétersbourg* (Evenings in Saint Petersburg), had made up the basic theme of the reactionary tradition. One cannot otherwise explain Verlaine's remarks against the Oratorians, his wild attack against Port-Royal in which he makes Pascal and gentle Pierre Nicole responsible for the Terror of '93, and describes the history of the Church of France exclusively as a function of the Society of Jesus. Similarly, Verlaine's conclusions on the Restoration, his notion of the irremediable decadence of France, may be found in exactly the same form in Barbey's *Prophètes du passé*; and one might justifiably say that Verlaine borrowed his ideas from that book if the same diatribes were not at the basis of a whole tradition. Nonetheless, it is now known that Barbey's book was a part of the poet's small library in Juniville.

Perhaps the most personal thing about this pamphlet is the nostalgic vision in which the poet delights. He imagines an ancien régime that is the faithful heir of a chivalrous, courtly, and heroic Middle Ages, and like all yearners after the past he clings to this illusion out of disgust with contemporary reality. In his eyes the France of 1880 represents the reign of weak and grasping mediocrity, the reign of money. It is not so much the populace he loathes, although he finds it corrupt and degraded, but the opportunistic Republican government, parliamentarianism, public life controlled by special interests. Historians have gotten into the habit of taking these political pages lightly. But Verlaine expounds views whose real significance became clear, some years later, in the Boulangist crisis. For the moment, the newly settled farmer of Juniville confines himself to praying quietly for civil war. "If a widespread revolt, for which one must hope and which one may properly expect from the Holy Spirit of the Lord of Hosts, were to rise up against present-day Filth," he wrote at the time. Certain violent statements in the last poems of *Sagesse*, in *Bonheur*, and in *Invectives* are not very clear except in the light of this *Voyage*.

When he returned to Paris in 1882, it was a prose work that, quite as much as the most beautiful of his poems, drew the attention of young literary men to Verlaine. From August 24, 1883, on, *Lutèce* began to bring out his *Poètes maudits*, a series of studies on Tristan Corbière, Rimbaud, and Mallarmé. Their influence, Laurent Tailhade said, spread like a train of gunpowder, exploded like fireworks, and transformed literary fashion overnight. Reading them today, one marvels at the stir they made at the time. This is for lack of understanding their import for the new generation. For all those who were determined not to fall victim to abhorrent academicism, and for all those who were no longer satisfied with Parnassian serenity, the only path left open at that time was a second-rate Baudelairianism, a poetry of the macabre and grotesque, a literature of neurosis of which Rollinat was the triumphant figurehead. Being modern meant sorrowing without hope, accommodating the ignoble, and a kind of naturalism that was more artificial and less serious than the contemporary pessimism delineated by Médan.

Verlaine had very deliberately made these *Poètes maudits* a call for a poetry of life and joy, equally distant from Parnassian artifice and the depressing modernities of naturalism. Against the Parnassians he wrote, on the very first page of *Poètes maudits*: "Nothing flawless, that is to say, boring." Against the graphic, interesting, but oh, so narrow Naturalists he puts up grace, the power of poetry, rhetoric in the great tradition. How can one possibly maintain that the doctrine that emerges from *Poètes maudits* is insignificant? To a literature that was either completely formalistic or plunged into a melancholy without issue, he proposed the very virtues it lacked

—the direct, sonorous, magistral flight, inspiration fierce and gentle by turns, the joy of a poetry that lived, laughed, struck through with the rays of the sun, of the moon, and the stars. He brought to it the ideal of a strong and simple language that could be brutal as well as charming, the ideal of a solidly grounded form of clean and lively line. It was this ideal, offered goodnaturedly but firmly and positively stated, that was responsible for the success of *Poètes maudits*. A second series, under the same title, containing studies of Marceline Desbordes-Valmore, Villiers, and Verlaine himself, came out from 1885 on. This series presented few new ideas, but it testified to the poet's faithfulness to a doctrine the Symbolists and Decadents repudiated.

Verlaine began very early to think of competing with Flaubert and the Goncourt brothers. In April 1873, he was devoting his thoughts to "a big intimate novel." He even claimed to have the work completely finished in his head. He died, however, without having written it. But he published a certain number of short prose pieces, mainly of autobiographical import, and the title be gave them—*Mémoires d'un veuf* (Memoirs of a Widower)—justifies seeking in them personal information and recollections. He had managed, in 1882, to contribute to *Réveil*. Four of his sketches were printed in the *Paris-Vivant* (Paris Today) column which Edmond Lepelletier had started. To make up his book, he added to these pieces some short prose poems in the style of Baudelaire, some personal recollections, and reflections on questions of the day. The assembled whole appeared under the title *Mémoires d'un veuf* in 1886.

This book enables us to understand Verlaine's position in regard to contemporary naturalism. In a more positive way than Alphonse Daudet, who was his *bête noire,* he provided the example of a tempered and gently ironical realism, of a faithfulness of observation that went hand in hand with an ever alert sensibility. He was neither brutal nor cruel. Yet he was as faithful to reality as the strictest of realists, and it has rightly been said that in his evocations of everyday and lower-class life, he strikes truer notes, he sees and describes better than Zola's best disciples.

At the time he was putting together selections for *Mémoires d'un veuf*, with the exception only of the most recently written pieces, Verlaine's prose was admirable in its delightful subtlety, a subtlety that did not lose itself in the excesses that would soon crop up in it. The writer adopted a language of childlike directness and charm, which flashed from time to time with a word of slang, a deliberate vulgarism, or a word corrupted in the Parisian accent. But these minor dissonances, sufficiently rare, do not lower the standard of the whole and only give it piquancy. A young Belgian writer managed, in 1886, to say the definitive words about this curious volume which is so badly understood and undervalued by critics today. "*Mémoires d'un veuf*," wrote Emile Verhaeren, "is a collection of delicate and fragile pictures through which runs a gentle breath of resignation." He had grasped that this casual prose—the idling of the eyes, of dreams, and steps, as he called it—was still and remained the poetry of *Fêtes galantes* and *Romances sans paroles*.

The same year as *Mémoires d'un veuf*, Verlaine published a collection of novelettes—*Louise Leclercq, Le Poteau*, and *Pierre Duchâtelet*. These texts show in a curious fashion the difficulty the writer experienced in giving life to his characters, in making them act and speak according to their own particular natures. *Louise Leclercq* is the story of a young girl who flees the paternal roof. We do not for an instant believe in this adventure. We have the impression throughout that the writer is talking about himself. This impression may be unjust. Perhaps Verlaine has himself in mind less than it seems. But his personality is so much present in his story that we are unable to forget it for an instant. The same fault is found in a prose drama, *Madame Aubin*, which he added to the book. Verlaine's talent, like Baudelaire's, is too subjective to create a novel or a living dramatic work.

In 1889, Verlaine had a collection of seven stories all ready for publication. He planned to call it *Histoires comme ça* (Just So Stories) and intended that Savine bring it out. This plan was not realized, and *Histoires comme ça* first appeared in periodicals. They were not collected until after the writer's death, in the volume of *Oeuvres posthumes*. One notes in them the same gifts of playful and alert observation as in *Mémoires d'un veuf,* the same impossibility, for Verlaine, of forgetting himself in order to give consistency to a story and to characters: his own life, his misfortunes, his dreams, show transparently through a lifeless plot and the shadowy figures he sketches. But one should perhaps remark that these stories, so far removed from naturalistic inspiration, have the merit, thanks to that vagueness the author deliberately maintains, of opening up areas of mystery, terror, or fantasy, of inviting the reader to dream a little.

In May 1891, *Echo de Paris* accepted a series of Verlaine's articles on the stays he had been making for the last five years in Paris hospitals. They were only an expanded version of a work the poet had revised at the end of 1890 and which, at that date, constituted a sheaf of twelve closely written pages. After appearing in the newspaper, they were collected in a book whose title was a gentle parody of Silvio Pellico's *Le mie prigioni:* Verlaine called them *Mes Hôpitaux* (My Hospitals).

This book did much to draw the attention of the general public to its author. One can only repeat in its favor the same remarks prompted by *Mémoires d'un veuf* and *Histoires comme ça.* It has the same quality of phrase, the same air of good nature, subtle banter, sly ingenuousness. As in the preceding volumes, the sentence is nimbly paced, varied in tone, elliptical, and free, but not at all disjointed. Consequently, it is a delightful work. But perhaps it puts its finger on an aspect of Verlaine's character that we tend not to notice today but which struck certain of his contemporaries—the refusal to look the tragic cast of his own life in the face, a kind of incurable childishness that enable him to dally over some amusing and curious detail at the very instant that he is in the process of slipping into the abyss. The first chapter of *Mes Hôpitaux* offers a striking example of this fact. When he comes to evoking the horrible distresses of 1887, far from lingering, he rushes his narrative: "An absolutely black interim. Misery and almost the hangman." These few words are enough for him, and he hastens to pass on to happier scenes.

Although the language in *Mes Hôpitaux* is still sharp and firm, one nonetheless observes certain sentences that are more overrefined than subtle, a number of excessive ellipses, obscurities. These faults are multiplied in the volume the writer brought out in 1892, and which he titled, after Pellico, *Mes Prisons* (My Prisons). It is not a matter of criticizing these pages—which appeared in *Chat Noir*—for the inaccuracies with which they teem; these may be explained for the most part by the inevitable mixings-up of an uncertain memory. But what is more serious is that the sentences have become disjointed, awkward, tortured, and overloaded. This is no longer the good nature of *Mémoires d'un veuf*. This is the simulated mischievousness of the facetious person who winks at you and hopes to draw a knowing smile out of you. Read, for instance, this sentence, similar to so many others in this mediocre book: "I wouldn't know how, naturally, to give an accurate account of them at this time when my maturer years are already upon me! after so many years and so many somewhat more serious bars to my freedom as a man for such and such reasons among which one must count precisely that abuse of the coupling in question above . . ."!

In the *Confessions*, which came out in book form in 1895, one no longer finds, or rarely finds, this disjointed type of sentence or this tangle of thought. One senses, it is true, that the narrative has been deliberately drawn out and that every opportunity for padding has been taken. This is all too well explained, although not the less excusable, when one knows that in June 1894, the author sold his unpublished *Confessions* to Edouard Dujardin at the rate of fifty centimes a line. Verlaine also too often employs that English turn of phrase which crams adjectives and adverbs between the article and the noun. But the wayward and dilatory manner of the *Confessions* makes it an engaging book, and one is sorry it ends so soon—right after the events of the Commune. One feels, on the part of the writer, a desire to convey in words not so much the material reality of events as the shimmering reflection in his mind of the places and men, the readings and adventures of which his life was woven. He spoke of a "battle with minutiæ to be expressed" and of the "almost infinitesmal nuances" he had to articulate. It is from that point of view that the *Confessions* should be read and savored.

These books of prose are only a portion of the prose work

written. There is a considerable amount. It is divided among narratives that are nearly always recollections, impressions from the past, and short critical studies. There are some Belgian sketches, some digressions dating from the Coulommes period and the last years in Paris, and descriptions of his various lodgings on the Left Bank. And, on the other hand, there are articles on contemporary writers, full of amusing sallies, mischievous and naughty remarks, but full as well of serious and firmly asserted ideas: the best of these are probably the biographies he wrote for the "Hommes d'aujourd'hui" series. Verlaine was not a great critic, for he was not interested in, and perhaps incapable of, developing an idea in a systematic manner. But a sentence here and there, an unexpected word, a felicitous adjective are sufficient proof that he felt and understood the strengths and weaknesses of works and men.

Conclusions

IN THE preceding pages an attempt has been made to record with accuracy the succession of events that marked Verlaine's life and to describe his works in detail. But minds are so constructed that they are not content with such descriptions and accounts. It is possible even that these latter begin to be of interest only if they lead to an overall view in which each detail falls into place within an original perspective, and if, by the same token, they make a value judgment possible.

That Verlaine the man is, because of his complexity, harder to understand than any other man becomes quite obvious when one reads the recent biographies. He is said to have a weak character. But this weakness is mingled with a sturdy tenaciousness, a toughness of mind that pushes him to the extreme consequences of his views and lends him, in more than one instance, the air of a doctrinaire and fanatic. Lepelletier tells us that in the Parnassian group he pursued the exigencies of impassiveness further than anyone. Similarly, although his friends were satisfied with being Republicans, he was an Hébertist and lent his support to the Commune more passionately than any of them. But when he was converted, he went to the blindest possible extremes in his diatribes against the modern mind and democracy.

He is said to have been incapable of settling on anything, of maintaining any particular resolve for any length of time. He was, on the contrary, astonishingly firm and persistent in the path he adopted. Until 1874 he was groping. But from that time on, that is, from his thirtieth year until his death, he stubbornly held fast to the definitive choice he had made. Stickney, Bournemouth, Rethel, Juniville, saw this man of contemplative mien pass along their roads, walking with rather unnatural solemnity, his hands crossed on his chest, the man the students in Rethel called Jesus Christ. Even after 1885 he changed less than people think. One should read the remarks that Byvanck took down in 1891, and the poems the poet composed in 1893 when a brush with death revived his former fervor. In practice his faithfulness to the original choice he made may have weakened. But the choice itself remained the same.

Similarly, the apparent impetuousness, the so-called impulsions that seem to direct his life conceal more often than not duly meditated projects. It is likely that his departure with Rimbaud in July 1872, was planned. It is even more likely that his departure from London in July 1873, was made in collusion with his mother. His seeming lack of stability after 1875 is misleading. He left Stickney because he was working there on ridiculous terms, and when he left he had been thinking about leaving for six months. He left Boston, not on impulse, but because he had been deceived about the work that awaited him there and because his situation was unendurable. During all these years, his "instability" did not in the least differ from that of teachers in private schools generally—and that kind of instability, although more marked than that of civil servants, is altogether usual, and there is no compelling reason to consider it other than perfectly matter of fact.

Let us not, therefore, be too hasty in calling Verlaine weak and unstable. Let us be even less eager to say he had a taste for adventure. It came into his life in spite of himself. A close look makes it appear certain that in July 1872, he had nothing more in mind than spending a few weeks in Fampoux with Rimbaud. It was in spite of himself that he went on to Belgium, and then to England. It was in spite of himself that his home was broken up. He dreamt constantly of some settled and peaceful situation—a civil servant post, a little plot of land to farm far from Paris, far from men of letters and false friends. When he returned to the capital with Lucien Létinois, those who met him were astonished by the prudence of his behavior and his words.

He praised the humanist Rollin while quietly drinking watered rum!

The mistake we too often make in attempting to understand and judge a life is to believe it to be entirely willed, that it was considered as a whole and consented to, or as modern jargon puts it, "assumed." The role of the unintentional, of the train of events, of compulsion, is great. In the case of Verlaine, it is overwhelming. His whole life was dominated by a very few unconsidered acts he committed and which he was wrong in doing; then when he came to his senses he did not recognize himself, but nevertheless those acts burdened his entire existence in relentless fashion. It was in vain that for eight years he effected an admirable reform; neither his wife nor society chose to believe in it. He regained neither home nor social position. If historians, instead of entertaining themselves by bringing into relief the fluctuations in his life, were to try to understand its basic concerns, they would perceive that from 1875 to 1883 Verlaine's efforts were directed to the goal of restoring his home and of making something of himself. But the limitations of his situation were in full play; he had no university degrees, he had no farming experience, and the only avenue reasonably open to him in fact—the Hôtel de Ville—was closed because extracts of the Brussels trial and the divorce decree were on his record.

Verlaine, therefore, did not elect, he did not will, the wretchedness of his last years. It was imposed on him. And new compulsions, moreover, kept him in this condition: the awful poverty in which he found himself plunged in January 1886, and the state of his health. One must be entirely ignorant of the life of men of letters in the nineteenth century not to know what difficulties those without an assured income had to struggle against, and how they had, consequently, to submit to the hard terms of magazine editors and publishers.

The situation in which Verlaine found himself plunged in 1886 is exactly like that of Barbey d'Aurevilly at one period in his life, and even more precisely like that of Villiers de l'Isle-Adam. What distinguishes Verlaine is the seriousness and tenacity of his endeavor to pull himself out of his poverty. Compare him to Léon Bloy. Whatever else one may think of him, even his friends could not help but deplore his laziness. Verlaine, on the contrary, wished to rectify a seemingly desperate situation—and, despite the condition of his health, he succeeded in doing so in the space of four years. From 1890 on, he was earning enough money to relieve him of any serious worry. Verlaine did not accept his deterioration until 1891, but at that time he was, physically, a doomed man.

Once one has dismissed certain long-standing errors about his character, and once the role of the constraints that burdened him has been determined, it remains to discover the features that specifically define his character. After collating the different evidence of those who actually knew him and who saw him often, one conclusion seems unavoidable: he was in everyday life a gentle, peaceful, fastidious man who observed the proprieties to an unusual and deliberately punctilious degree. This is Lepelletier's and Delahaye's opinion; it is the impression he first gave Mathilde, and the reputation he had among men of letters. These qualities persisted through his very last years; Rachilde, Cazals, Le Rouge, and Raynaud agree on this point. Any picture of Verlaine that does not stress this gentleness, propriety, and fastidiousness should be considered a caricature.

This is not to say that he did not have his faults. But his failings are not those that have been most dwelled on. He was greedy, like a child. He was rather more than reticent, he was close and, to put it bluntly, sneaky. Finally, he was not a brave man and preferred to watch others fight rather than run risks himself. These last two faults sometimes attained unfortunate proportions. In order to keep something a secret, he would lie. The letters in which he speaks of his household and of Rimbaud were written, not to relate the truth, but to conceal it. Those who did not like him said he had a "crooked" side. This is a frightfully harsh word. But it is justified, so long as one takes fully into account that Verlaine deceives, not for the pleasure of deceiving, but to protect himself, to prevent others from learning his secret. Similarly, because he lacked courage, he was cowardly, and this cowardice figured among the causes of his misfortunes. The Verlaine who fled to Belgium and trailed after Rimbaud to England was a frightened Verlaine. The historians who point out the frequent discrepancy between his rather heroic professions of faith and the extreme timidity of his behavior do not lack evidence, alas, for seeing in this a fresh proof of his duplicity.

But it is not because he was greedy or inherently reticent and timorous, it is not for these reasons that Verlaine's life was marked by grievous misfortunes. It is because in certain moments of crisis actual fits of insanity came over him, convulsing his ordinarily peaceful life, sweeping away good resolutions, blasting his efforts at recovery. What we know of his life proves that he had attacks of this sort in 1869, 1872, and in 1885. It is quite possible and probable that there were others. Philomène undoubtedly had her reasons for calling him "the Devil himself."

Of the nature of these attacks, let us not deceive ourselves; we know very little about them. They were usually tied up with drunkenness, but one has the impression that they were not simply due to alcohol. It appears rather that Verlaine exorcised through absinthe the demons that possessed him. Is one to believe that these seizures were an expression of the intensity of some desire thwarted by the obstacles it encountered? Or did they derive from some anguish, from that kind of vertigo certain men experience when they feel they have lost or are about to lose the object responsible at that moment for their entire happiness? Might not these fits of madness be nothing more, in his case, than fear, the awful fear of finding himself facing the abyss of life alone? One more readily believes the last explanation. The 1869 attack appears to follow the death of his father and the even more recent death of Elisa Moncomble. Certain evidence proves that one of Verlaine's characteristic traits was his inability to endure solitude, that he needed to feel someone near. One should observe, too, that the Brussels affair is not easy to account for by transports of desire and is much better accounted for by the fact that in the future Rimbaud intended to leave his friend alone.

In the face of this long endeavor of a man to put his life on an orderly, rational basis, in the face of his persistence in rebuilding this structure every time a storm knocked it down, one feels the flagrant injustice of certain judgments. One sees that it is impossible to despise this unfortunate man and that

he much more properly deserves our admiration. Why, however, are we obliged to distinguish, even in his strivings for
good, something equivocal and dubious? When he humbles
himself, when he confesses himself a sinner, there is still something suspect about it all, something that brings Tartuffe to
mind. At the same time that he is bragging about having become "completely softened toward others, completely submis-
sive to The Other" (meaning God), he writes about the unfortunate Mathilde: "The little minx must be made to choke
on her own spittle." It appears that he does not remember
these hateful outbursts; perhaps he lies to himself. In any
case, he lies to us. His endeavors, we now know, were sincere,
and his convictions genuine. At the same time, however, there
was posing and showing off. How could a wholly honest man
write: "I am altogether gentle and completely naïve. . . ."
What excuse can one possibly find for Mathilde's former husband, Rimbaud's friend, the author of *Hombres* and *Femmes*,
when in his later years he speaks of and dares write of the
"solemn turn of mind from which I have since then but rarely
wandered"!

That is probably where the essential feature of Verlaine's
psychology may be seen. For the outbursts, which were the
origin of his troubles, remain, so to speak, exterior; they over-
power him, they sweep him off his feet, and then when the
storm has passed, he considers, without much understanding,
the damage that has been done. But that his striving toward
good cannot be considered apart from a need to pose, to show
off before others, that is what defines and reveals his true
nature, his most secret law. With him everything is referent
to other people. Morality was presented to him, from child-
hood, as an aggregate of precepts laid down by his parents, the
Paliseul family, and the priests. His moral sense never developed beyond that point. When he strayed from these precepts,
he was rebelling, with all the guiltiness of conscience that word
implies. When he repented, it was to bow down before the
rules from which he had in vain attempted to free himself. The
rebellious child one moment, the obedient child the next, he
never stopped being a child. His childish conscience seeks ap-

proval or disapproval from others; it tries to adapt to the permissive image it wants to read in their eyes.

Many have testified that Verlaine was a child all his life. Lantoine admired his "marvelously childlike" gaze. Byvanck noted the childlike changeableness of his face. Cazals made amusing sketches of his old friend in boyish poses, and Léon Bloy wrote to Father Dewez: "You cannot have any idea of the childishness of this highly unhappy man." One must make the best of it. The inscrutable-looking Verlaine, posing with lordly authoritative gaze for the photographers, is Verlaine as he wished us to see him, as he pretends to see himself. One cannot say that he is deceiving us simply because he wants to be that particular man. But he is not that man and never will be. It is this basic childishness which explains why so many genuine, persistent, courageous efforts could never be free of disquieting ambiguousness and why they so often gave the impression of being nothing but show and deceit.

If Verlaine the man is hard to understand, the poet and artist present no less an uncertainty, which is reflected in the books devoted to his work. For some years he was considered the greatest of living poets. He undoubtedly is still one of the most widely read, one of the few poets who have attained a general audience in France. But he has, perhaps, had no influence on the development of French poetry. Mallarmé and Rimbaud, much more than he, have dominated the sixty years that have passed since his death. Valéry extended the teaching of the former, the surrealists took over the legacy of the latter. As for the theorists, the hostile position taken about him by Charles Maurras caused many others to adopt a disdainful attitude. André Breton has said that the author of *Sagesse* should be left to little girls in the provinces and is no better or worse than Samain, while a well-known follower of Maurras insisted he was not fit for inclusion in an anthology of French poetry. The contrast between Verlaine's reputation among readers and critics is certainly striking and reveals bias. But the above is only an extreme form of what seems to be a general reticence. One still cannot say that it is generally accepted that Verlaine was a great poet.

There should, however, be no doubt of it. Verlaine has that primary and rare virtue of handling the resources of the language with supreme mastery. He has none of the difficulty of expression one detects in Vigny, in Baudelaire's earliest poems, and which is apparent in some of Mallarmé's poems. He did write some bad poems; but this was never from lack of talent but rather from too daring brevity, or overrefinement, or finally, from the economy of expression he deliberately forced on himself. Although it is true that his inspiration "depoetized" itself sometimes, and more and more often with the years, it remained to the end inquisitive and acute.

Some criticize him for being merely a pleasant poet. Jules Romains, for the further glorification of his mentor Moréas, wrote in *Les Hommes de bonne volonté* (Men of Good Will): "How pleasant and anecdotal Verlaine's distress seems by comparison!" This description is patently and completely unjust. Neither Moréas nor anyone else wrote more poignant, more bitter, or more powerful verses than some of the poems in *Sagesse*. It is quite true that the inspiration, in Verlaine's case, does not consistently have the taut quality of *Fleurs du Mal*, that one often detects in him, in his relaxed moments, a soft and contented view of life, that it takes storms and vertigoes to lift him to a certain sublimity of emotion. But it is enough that from time to time a shattering outcry cuts through his work that his greatness be acknowledged.

If these very simple truths are not more widely acknowledged, it is because we too often judge Verlaine's genius only by his early collections. He is for too many people the author only of *Fêtes galantes* and *Romances sans paroles*. His reputation is still bound to the tremendous success of these exquisite works. People ignore the fact that in the spring of 1873, when he had only just finished *Romances sans paroles*, he was already dissatisfied with it and contemplated a more difficult and loftier work.

If we look closely, we see that Verlaine's fortune is linked to that of impressionism, and that the things the critics reproach him for are exactly the same things for which our contemporaries criticize painters of the Impressionist school. Critics claim that he did not go beyond ephemeral and subjective impressions, that he confined himself to reporting them, and that he was incapable of rising any higher. But this criticism is false, absolutely false. For, as a matter of fact, as we have seen, the author of *Sagesse* broke away from impressionism; he very quickly became aware of its inadequacies, and from 1873 on, he undertook to rediscover the great romantic lyric line, wherein the drama of our destiny is unfolded through an expansive flood of images.

Let us examine, moreover, the line of argument of other of Verlaine's detractors, the criticism they level at his work. The grievance they harbor against him is that of having dealt a blow to the intellect, of having sinned against Minerva, of having delivered French poetry over to all the false marvels of an obscure intuitionism. But it is not true that the value of a poet's work is a function of the gratification it gives to the intellect, and it is possible for Verlaine to be a very great poet without bringing us anything more than the authentic expression of his marvelous and tormented soul. Because he bore within himself a whole world of dreams, the yearning for lost paradises, because his life was one long drama of anguish, of despair and hope, his work touches in us not those superficial regions illumined by the cold light of the intellect, but that part of us that is at once most hidden and most genuine, the area in which we confront our own life in the most immediate and pure consciousness of its being.

Furthermore, what errors of fact there are in the interpretations of Verlaine that link him with particular schools of poetry! He is so much alone! Should one call him a Symbolist? But there are no little girls with luxuriant heads of hair, no crystalline lakes, no mysterious swans in his work. No poisonous flesh or flowers of murderous scent. At one time he did write a few lines for the *Revue wagnérienne.* But he was the first to laugh about it: "a vaguely loony sonnet . . ." he wrote. Will one link his work with the Decadent school? But he remains wholly unacquainted with Schopenhauer and makes fun of contemporary pessimists. No philosophy could make him acknowledge that life is illusion and that man is nothing but a simulacrum of idea. He could see "Germanism," as he called it, in this metaphysics.

He is, indeed, more purely French than any other poet. He lived at a time when people in France were enthusiastically caught up in Ibsen, Tolstoi, and Dostoievski. Verlaine was not in the least sympathetic to this vogue. He was wrong, moreover, and it is not to pay him a compliment that his attitude is here recorded. It is rather to indicate the degree to which he remained apart from the cosmopolitan cast of mind that was one of the most salient features of Decadence in the ordinary sense of the word.

What should be said rather is that he did not firmly enough resist the pitfalls of an age in confusion. The influence he exercised over the young generation of 1885 has been mentioned. It would be well, too, to study the influence that generation had on him, on his language, on his prosody. If, at the time of *Bonheur*, his sentences become disjointed, if his choice of words carries his scorn for proper usage to extremes, it is because he has allowed himself to be led astray and that, as head of the young poets, he thinks it his duty to follow them. What proves that he moved in this direction reluctantly is the fact that in 1892, when he had broken off with his friends, abandoned all groups, abdicated from his position as leader of a coterie, his poetry righted itself and returned once more to that purity of line it had before 1882.

He was responsible, with others, for the breaking-up of the traditional forms of French poetry. But all major renascences pay this price. The Pléiade began by holding up to ridicule the lyric verse forms commended to them by time-honored tradition. The first generation of Romantics first cast aside the tropes of classic lyricism and the whole stock of words and turns of phrase with which their contemporaries had come to associate the idea of poetry. And it was because a new rhetoric had been born, because new methods had been imposed on the poet's vision that Verlaine grasped the urgent need for a new liberating effort.

The essential thing about his work is not, moreover, its prosodic innovations or its relaxation of the rules. If he is fond of new meters, if he arranges his rhymes freely, if he sometimes does violence to the language, it is not because of his inability to endure discipline, it is because he understood, better than others, that poetry is the quivering of the soul, which is more deeply embedded in man than intellect, and that rational structures can only hamper spiritual impulse.

In that, he was only reiterating one of the governing ideas of Romanticism. An idea that Novalis, Tieck, Hölderin, and others like them had grasped in one fell swoop, but which gained ground in France all too slowly. From Lamartine's *Méditations* to his *La Chute d'un ange* (Fall of an Angel), from Hugo's *Odes* to the volumes of his last period, we are witness to the progressive discovery of a poetry that frees man's spirit and gives him direct awareness of existence in all its fullness and momentum. Nodier, Nerval, and, more than any, Baudelaire, understood that the poet opens the doors of illusion and penetrates those mysterious regions that are not lit by reason. Verlaine followed after these precursors, pushing further, but always in the same direction. And his accomplishment is undoubtedly that of having worked out their principles in language and in prosody. One may claim, without being unjust to Nerval and Baudelaire, that the means of expression in their work remains traditional to too great a degree and that, bearers of a new concept of the art of poetry, they did not manage to find the new forms it demanded. Verlaine understood better than they the necessity for this renewal.

Such is the position he occupies in the history of French poetry. Far from being merely the last manifestation of worn-out poetics—as it has today become common custom to describe it—one must see his work as a stage in the route that leads, within the bounds of the ninteenth century, from the rhymed rhetoric of the imperial period to the authentic poetry of Claudel and Apollinaire. This, of course, is a historical view, and consequently one that has the fault of seeing the historical significance of this work rather than its intrinsic value. As for the latter, what proof can one offer those who refuse to acknowledge it? And what more can one say to men of good will other than that they reread those marvelous pages into which the poet of *Fêtes galantes* and *Romances sans paroles*, into which the prisoner of Mons and the humble solitary of Stickney put his dreams, his misery, and his hopes.

A *Selected List*

I. EDITIONS

For Verlaine's complete output, verse and prose: The edition of *Oeuvres complètes* (Complete Works), 5 vols., and the edition of *Oeuvres posthumes* (Posthumous Works) in 3 vols., published by Messein, Paris.

For his works in verse: The Pléiade edition, published by Gallimard. This volume has the advantage of providing all information known on the date of each selection, a list of printed variants and even, on occasion, manuscript variants. But H. de Bouillane de Lacoste's edition of *Bonheur* revealed to what degree Verlaine's printed texts abound with errors and demonstrated the absolute necessity of going back to the manuscripts.

The edition of the *Oeuvres complètes* (Complete Works), 2 vols., published by the Club du Meilleur Livre, 1959–1960. The text, established by the late H. de Bouillane de Lacoste, with an introduction by O. Nadal, is presented with excellent commentary and notes by Jacques Borel.

There are critical editions of some of the individual collections. Three of these editions provide a model for the work that is urgently needed on the complete output. They are: H. de Bouillane de Lacoste's edition of *Bonheur*, J. H. Bornecque's *Poèmes saturniens*, and his *Fêtes galantes*, Librairie Nizet, Paris, 1960.

The *Correspondance* has been edited in three volumes by

Ad. von Bever, published by Messein. The text is correct, but many letters are dated wrongly, and the task of collecting the very numerous letters that either have been published only in various periodicals or have not yet appeared in print at all remains undone.

II. BIOGRAPHICAL STUDIES

In 1938 an excellent brief book of introduction and bibliography, *L'Etat présent des études verlainiennes* (The Present State of Verlaine Studies), by Claude Cuénot was published by Editions des Belles Lettres. This is still the best study tool for anyone who wishes to grapple with Verlaine's life and work.

On Verlaine's life two accounts dominate all others: that of Edmond Lepelletier, *Paul Verlaine, sa vie, son oeuvre* (Paul Verlaine, His Life, His Work), *Mercure de France*, 1923; and that of Ernest Delahaye, *Verlaine*, 1919. Delahaye also published *Souvenirs familiers à propos de Verlaine, Rimbaud et Germain Nouveau* (Intimate Recollections about Verlaine, Rimbaud, and Germain Nouveau), 1925. Despite gaps that are all too easily accounted for, these are candid works written by men who knew the poet intimately.

To these accounts should be added, for various periods of his life:

Madame Delporte (formerly Verlaine), *Mémoires de ma vie* (Recollections of My Life), 1935.

F. A. Cazals and G. Le Rouge, *Les derniers jours de P. Verlaine* (The Last Days of P. Verlaine), 1923.

Ch. Donos, *Verlaine intime* (The Inner Verlaine), 1898.

Ernest Raynaud, "Les portraits de Verlaine" (Portraits of Verlaine), *Mercure de France*, August 15, 1906.

The February 1, 1943, issue of *Nouvelle Revue française* printed a number of important texts taken from police files. These were subsequently brought together in a booklet.

Extremely valuable information may be found in J. M. Carré's *Du côté de Verlaine et de Rimbaud* (With Verlaine and Rimbaud), 1949, with reproductions of the drawings kept in the Doucet library.

The drawings and photographs collected in *L'Iconographie*

verlainienne (The Verlaine Iconography), by Fr. Ruchon, Geneva, 1947, are of great value.

Of the studies devoted to Verlaine, the best known is *Verlaine tel qu'il fut* (Verlaine as He Was), by François Porché (Flammarion). He is a gifted biographer. But it is not enough to say that his book is defamatory. It should be understood, especially, that in his desire to reach the general public through a highly colored narrative, Porché has systemtically distorted the truth, exaggerated the facts, and aimed for false pathos. To take but one example, he pays no attention to the accounts of Verlaine's death and presents it in a totally fanciful light, one which, to his mind, will more powerfully affect the reader than the truth. When it is a question of denigrating Verlaine, he takes liberties with the text verging on falsification. I have given one enlightening example of this in an article, "A propos d'une citation" (In Regard to a Quotation), in *La Grive*, June 1945.

Marcel Coulon's two works: *Au coeur de Verlaine et de Rimbaud* (At the Heart of Verlaine and Rimbaud), 1925, and *Verlaine, poète saturnien* (Verlaine: Saturnine Poet), 1929, take their stand from too harsh a point of view. But they contain valuable bits of information and are still worth consulting.

If our understanding of Verlaine has been changed since 1930, it is thanks to a number of short studies. Here are the most notable ones:

Léon Le Fefve de Vivy's book, *Les Verlaine* (The Verlaine Family), Brussels, 1928, on the paternal side of Verlaine's family and its ties in the Ardennes area.

On the maternal side of Verlaine's family—the Dehées from Arras and Fampoux—we have had up to this time only a few vague particulars. We are now well informed, thanks to the research M. P. Bougard, chief archivist of Pas-de-Calais, consented to do for this volume, the results of which were printed in *Revue des sciences humaines*, April–June 1952.

On Verlaine's studies at the Lycée Bonaparte, all the data is given in an article by Léon Lemonnier, *Grande Revue*, vol. III, 1924.

On Verlaine's visits to England, there is one remarkable work by V. P. Underwood, *Verlaine et l'Angleterre* (Verlaine and England), a thesis defended before the Faculté des Lettres of

Lille in February 1950, and published in 1956 by Librairie Nizet. One should refer as well to the following articles by Underwood:

"Chronologie des lettres anglaises de Verlaine" (A Chronology of Verlaine's English Letters), *Revue de littérature comparée*, July–September 1938.

"Chronologie verlainienne" (Verlaine Chronology), *Revue d'histoire de la philosophie*, Lille, January 1938.

"Le *Cellulairement* de Paul Verlaine" (Paul Verlaine's *Cellulairement*), *Revue d'histoire littéraire*, July–September 1938.

"Verlaine et Létinois en Angleterre" (Verlaine and Létinois in England), *Mercure de France*, June 1, 1938.

Underwood has published a "Carnet personnel de Verlaine" (Verlaine's Personal Notebook) in *Revue des sciences humaines*, 1955.

G. Vanwelkenhuysen's book, *Verlaine en Belgique* (Verlaine in Belgium), contains unpublished documents and valuable accounts, especially on the poet's travels as a lecturer.

III. STUDIES OF THE WORK

In 1926, Ad. van Bever and Maurice Monda published (by Messein) a *Bibliographie et iconographie de Paul Verlaine* (A Bibliography and Iconography of Paul Verlaine), which gives a complete list of Verlaine's publications, including pieces that appeared in periodicals and in book form. They failed, however, to list the publication of six of the poems from *Fêtes galantes* in *L'Artiste*.

Amazing as it may seem, we do not have the great comprehensive study that Verlaine's work merits. Pierre Martino's *Verlaine*, Hatier-Boivin, 1924, is full of fine things but does not pretend to be the definitive work we still lack.

Two studies that permit us to hope for an end to this unsatisfactory situation in the near future are J. H. Bornecque's annotated edition of *Poèmes saturniens* and his very important article on *Fêtes galantes* printed in *Mélanges Mornet*, Librairie Nizet, 1951.

On the problems posed by *Cellulairement*, one should consult E. Dupuy's article, "Etude critique sur le texte d'un manuscrit de Paul Verlaine" (Critical Study of the Text of a

Paul Verlaine Manuscript), *Revue d'histoire littéraire*, 1913; and, for the opposite point of view, the article by Underwood cited above.

On the influence of English poetry in Verlaine's work, Underwood's thesis records the results of close and extensive research. He has brought to light Verlaine's debt to the Anglican liturgy.

Verlaine has been studied from the viewpoint of Catholic theology by Charles Morice: *Verlaine, le drame religieux* (Verlaine, the Religious Drama), 1946.

Since the first printing of the present work, the Verlaine bibliography has been enriched by a fine volume by J. Richer: *Paul Verlaine*, in the "Poètes d'aujourd'hui" series. It offers a number of unpublished documents. These have been taken into account in this new printing wherever these texts altered the traditional version of the facts or generally accepted dates.

To be read with equally great interest is an article by Jean Richer, "Repaires et documents verlainiens" (Verlaine References and Records), published in the June 1, 1954, issue of *Mercure de France*; and Roger A. Lhombreaud's "Verlaine et ses amis d'Angleterre" (Verlaine and His English Friends), in *Revue d'histoire littéraire*, July–September 1953. *Lettres de Huysmans à Zola* (Huysmans' Letters to Zola), published by Pierre Lambert, with Droz et Giard, contains several extremely valuable pieces of information about the year 1888. A letter from Verlaine to Matuszewicz, which passed unnoticed in *Revue historique de l'armée* in 1946, was published again in the June 1, 1953, issue of *Mercure de France*. It is authoritative as regards the "week in Brussels" in 1873.

In the issue of *Empreintes* devoted to Verlaine one may read a very fine letter by Max Elskamp on the subject of one of Verlaine's lectures. It describes him as "so gentle, so simple, so good, it appears, and so awkward as well." This testimony will undoubtedly grieve those who prefer to picture Verlaine as a consistently degraded man.

Since the last printing of this book, several articles have appeared to which one may easily find reference in the listings of *Revue d'histoire littéraire* and of *Studi francesi*. A few books have made basic contributions to Verlaine studies: the edition

of the *Oeuvres complètes* with commentary by Jacques Borel;
J. H. Bornecque's *Lumières sur les Fêtes galantes* (Lights on
Fêtes galantes); and V. P. Underwood's *Verlaine et l'Angleterre*. To the list of outstanding publications given above, one
should add G. Zayed's *Lettres inédites à Cazals* (Unpublished
Letters to Cazals), Droz, 1957, a model of graceful and fault-
less scholarship.

A NOTE ON VERLAINE TRANSLATIONS

There are three translations of Verlaine's poems readily available in English. All are selected volumes. Two can be recom-
mended. C. F. MacIntyre's *Paul Verlaine: Selected Poems* contains the French texts of seventy-nine poems from six of Verlaine's books. The translations, with the French on facing
pages, use meter and rhyme and stay close to the literal sense
of the originals. *Baudelaire, Rimbaud, Verlaine: Selected Verse
and Prose Poems,* edited with an Introduction by Joseph M.
Bernstein, contains a selection of sixty-six poems from seven
of Verlaine's books. The French text is not printed. Some of
Gertrude Hall's versions give a genuine feeling of Verlaine's
originals and are at the same time good English poems. This
is not true, however, of the Arthur Symons translations of
twenty poems from *Parallèlement* in the same volume.

C. M.

THE GOTHAM LIBRARY

Oscar Cargill, General Editor

Robert J. Clements, Associate Editor for Modern Languages

*A paperback series devoted to the major figures in world litera-
ture and topics of enduring importance*

*If these titles are not available at your bookstore, you may
order them by sending a check or money order direct to:* New
York University Press, 32 Washington Place, New York 3, New
York. *The Press will pay postage.*